BECAUSE NETIQUETTE MATTERS!

BECAUSE NETIQUETTE MATTERS!

Your Comprehensive Reference Guide

to E-mail Etiquette and

Proper Technology Use

Judith Kallos

To order additional copies of this book, contact:
Xlibris Corporation
1-888-795-4274
www.Xlibris.com
Orders@Xlibris.com
24220

CONTENTS

Don't Be An Online Knucklehead 13

Courtesy No. 1: Get To Know The Basics! 15

Courtesy No. 2: Perception Is The Only
    Reality Online 30

Courtesy No. 3: Proofread And Check For Errors 32

Courtesy No. 4: Be Sure To Sign Off 34

Courtesy No. 5: Instant Messaging Tips 37

Courtesy No. 6: Respond Promptly And Down Edit 41

Courtesy No. 7: Thou Shall Not Spam 45

Courtesy No. 8: You Are What You Write 50

Courtesy No. 9: Say No To Trolls 54

Courtesy No. 10: The Human Touch 57

Are You A Technology Mushroom? 59

The Scoop On Files 67

Cyberparenting 101 75

Business E-mail Basics 78

Using Signature Files 87

How To Deal With Rude E-mailers 92

Ten E-mail Organization Tips 97

Think Before You Forward 102

How To Identify And Handle Spam/UCE 104

Tips To Stop Spam! 111

How Not To Look Spammy 117

All About Viruses 120

To E-card Or Not To E-card 127

Domain Slamming 130

Take The Technology Challenge 136

Something's Phishy 144

HTML E-mail And Your Privacy 148

Cookies—No Fat, Zero Calories? 151

Approaching Employers Online 155

How To Search Better 158

Newbie F.A.Q. 160

Common E-mail Acronyms 168

Common E-mail Emoticons 170

Internet Glossary 172

Index 183

In memory of my father,
William Kallos,
who brought me up to know that only hard work
and personal responsibility can lead to success.
Thank you to my Paul,
a truly great man,
who without his suggestions,
unending support and love for the past 15 years,
I would have never gone down this technology path
well before most.
And after all the nerves and hopes in writing this book;
to my little dog Spike—
whose adorable face looking up at me
through my glass desk reminds me each day
that it is the simple things that makes one truly happy.

NETIQUETTE DEFINITION:

Using technology effectively to communicate with others, both personally and professionally with knowledge, understanding, and courtesy.

From e-mail etiquette and attachments, to misunderstandings and dilemmas, I have been available since the start of the Webolution to answer Netizen's e-mails personally and to offer my experience and advice. This book was created based on requests from the visitors to my Web site who desired a way of learning the basics of what participating online demands of each of us in a hard copy, off-line reference guide. Visitors also asked for a hard-copy reference guide that could be purchased as gifts for loved ones, used for employee training, or to assist community-organization members who are online or just getting online and are not yet aware of the importance of Netiquette issues. This book covers all the bases!

This comprehensive current guide covers it all from the most important points and themes, which are repeated throughout this book, to the little details that make a big impact. Those who do a complete read through of *Because Netiquette Matters!* will then clearly understand the importance of those issues, while at the same time those that prefer to use this book as a reference guide as situations arise will not miss the important details that relate to several specific topics. In covering e-mail etiquette issues, such as forwarding silly jokes and virus warnings, to typing in all caps or not using proper punctuation and grammar, I will cover each of these topics for you with clarity from both personal and business perspectives so that you know the importance and nuances of each.

Absorbing and then practicing the information and resources included in this book will, without a doubt, contribute to you being perceived as an individual that other onliners will want to communicate with and get to know better. Good Netiquette skills will ensure a pleasurable experience for all those whom you come in contact with online. Understand that other Netizens will only have your e-mail and how you use technology to form an opinion about you as a person. You don't want to be viewed as an *online knucklehead,* do you?

If you are online for commercial gain, use e-mail at your place of employment, or are planning on putting up a commercial Web site in the future, these issues will be critical to your level of success. Many new to the online world, as well as a healthy amount of those who have been online for some time, may feel that the issues that are covered in this book are an opinion or something they can ignore and minimize the importance of. Believe this at your own peril! When online, perception is the only reality. You should never underestimate the power of perception!

Not using common courtesies or reflecting a basic command of the technology in which you are participating will ensure others will probably not have a positive impression of you. As you know, impressions are everything! Lack of Netiquette efforts may also cause potential friends, associates, or customers to speculate what else you don't get and cringe when they see your name in their inbox. The last thing you will want is to be perceived as lazy or uneducated in regard to your communication skills and use of technology if you want to thrive online. This is a perception that can be the kiss of death for any online enterprise, and wouldn't that be a shame when that outcome can be completely avoided by simply relying on this book as your guide?

Many of the issues in this book are common sense, while others require only a little extra effort on your part. Newbies (a nickname with a negative connotation for those new to the online world) are many times not aware that these issues even exist to realize their importance. In addition, many online do not realize that these skills require ongoing diligence to be honed. With the combination of this book and the constantly updated and growing OnlineNetiquette.com, now everyone has access to this important information—on or offline!

Online, ignorance is not bliss. In a world where lack of personal accountability or the "anything goes" attitude prevails, your commitment to refining your command of Netiquette issues as well as communication and technology skills will go a long way in making it clear you are a person who made it out of the sixth grade, who is tech savvy and courteous and destined to be a success. And best of all, a pleasure to communicate with! You want to be perceived as the kind of person one would want to form a relationship with, share ideas and inspirations, and even possibly do business with. This book will help you do just that! If we are all on the same virtual page so to speak, the online world will be a much better place for all of us!

Please do not hesitate to contact me about your Netiquette issues by visiting my Netiquette Discussion Forums @ http://www.NetiquetteForums.com.

Wishing you abundant online success! ;-)

Virtually,
Judith
Your Netiquette Muse.

DON'T BE AN ONLINE KNUCKLEHEAD

Common courtesy, social graces, and socially acceptable behavior are all terms used in a civilized society where human beings interact with one another. Cyberspace is not any different and in particular has always been a self-governing society. How you will be perceived, the type of person that you are or, for that matter, are not, your credibility, your level of professionalism and ethics will be judged by how you communicate with others online.

Do you type in all caps? Do you refrain from using proper punctuation or grammar because you don't think it is necessary? Or do you forward every e-mail you believe to be funny or that says "forward to all your friends" to family and associates? Worse yet, do you list the e-mail addresses of those you are sending to all in the **To** field even though everyone you are sending to may not know each other? These are just a few of the topics I will cover for you.

To minimize the importance of established Netiquette guidelines or to think they do not apply to you is to make a conscious decision to most likely be thought of as rude, lazy, arrogant, and/or uneducated. If you are online for commercial gain, lack of proper Netiquette may very well deter those who otherwise may have considered doing business with you. You know why? Because Netiquette matters!

This is not frivolous commentary; this is not one person's opinion (although I am known for injecting my personality into the issue). This book is not in existence to call you names or make you feel bad. Quite the contrary! My hope is to empower you with the issues you need to know about and the skills you need to hone to be considered someone that when online people will want to communicate with. After all, you only need begin your online journey with . . .

Ten common courtesies . . .

COURTESY NO. 1

GET TO KNOW THE BASICS!

These online basics are minimally what you should become familiar with, absorb, and practice in order to be taken seriously in your online communications and use of technology.

1. **Do not type in all caps.** This is considered yelling or screaming online. Those who type in caps are perceived as lazy, uneducated, and not being considerate of those they communicate with who will have to read their e-mail. Various studies on the topic reflect that it is more difficult and takes longer to read text that is typed in all caps. And for those who question "What studies?" here is one example for your reading pleasure:

    http://www.psych.utoronto.ca/~muter/pmuter1.htm

    "Searching for words is faster with uppercase characters, but reading of continuous text is slower (Vartabedian, 1971), perhaps because interline masking is greater with uppercase (Nes, 1986). In addition, lowercase enhances reading efficiency because word shape is helpful in word recognition (Rudnicky & Kolers, 1984)."

    One is free, at his/her convenience, to review the entire document above, which goes into further detail.

Stating certain professions are required to type in all caps (That's the first time I've heard that one!) and therefore that applies to e-mail doesn't jive either. Would you send any off-line communication in all caps?—the answer is probably no. If your profession dictates all caps in certain situations, e-mail certainly is not one of them.

2. **Refrain from formatting your e-mail with colored text and background colors/images.** If I had one dollar for every Netizen who e-mailed me griping about how they cannot read e-mails that are formatted apparently by those who have no color sense, I could retire. Your color choices can make your e-mails impossible to decipher without having to go through extra steps to convert them to something readable. In addition, many times, when those you communicate with reply, they have to deal with your formatting carrying over to their reply—what a pain in the neck! Why would you expect others to have to go through that just to read and respond to your e-mail? The answer: many won't! Using large background graphics that take forever to download, especially if you connect via a modem through a phone connection (which is more common than most think once you get outside of most metropolitan areas), is plain old inconsiderate. If you do feel the uncontrollable need to use any type of formatting, do so sparingly. Please, on behalf of all those who e-mail me, just send your e-mails in plain text! When it comes to "plain" text, keep it plain. Don't turn all the text into colors and/or italics—both alone or combined make your e-mail more difficult to read.

3. **On those rare occasions where sending a group of people** the very same e-mail is necessary, more importantly if they do not know each other, as a courtesy to those you are sending to, please list all of the recipients' e-mail addresses in the **BCC** field. Blind Carbon Copy is from the

old days when typewriters used carbon paper to create identical copies of a document when it was being typed without recipients knowing who else received a copy. When an e-mail address is designated in the blind-carbon-copy field, the recipient will get a copy of the e-mail while their e-mail address remains invisible to the other recipients of the e-mail—some of whom they may or may not know. If you are not sure how to BCC in your e-mail program, here are site resources that may help you learn the features of your particular software programs:

OPERA: http://www.opera.com/support/

EUDORA: http://www.eudora.com/techsupport/

NETSCAPE: http://home.netscape.com/products/

OUTLOOK EXPRESS: http://support.microsoft.com/

Long lists of e-mail addresses at the beginning of any e-mail is an immediate sign that the sender is either a novice or a newbie and doesn't care to respect other's privacy. Neither of which are complimentary perceptions! E-mail addresses are like phone numbers. Only the owners of the e-mail address or phone number should be the one to authorize whom they want to have it and make it public to. Many onliners prefer to decide themselves who has their e-mail address.

The only time you would keep addresses visible is when a small group of onliners (up to five), who all have met in person, need to be on the same page. These onliners all know each other, and because the event or activity involves all of them, the **CC** field reflects who has been included in the e-mail, so all are aware of who was informed. As a good rule of thumb, if your e-mail address is in the **CC** field, you are being kept in the loop and not required to respond. Only those whose e-mail addresses are included in the **To** field are expected to respond. If you are not 100 percent sure that all those you are sending to wouldn't mind their e-mail addresses being made public to the other recipients, then don't publicize their addresses—use the **BCC** option.

By sending mass mails to a long list of visible e-mail addresses, you have made the decision to publicize your friend's and associate's e-mail addresses for them, which is not a good thing to do. Let those you correspond with determine for themselves whom they will make their e-mail address known to—do not make that decision for them. By listing handfuls of e-mail addresses in the e-mail headers for all to see is inconsiderate of each recipient's right to privacy. However, by having the knowledge and courtesy to list them in the **BCC** field when it is not required for all to know who else has been sent the same e-mail, you will show a command of technology and a respect for other's privacy. This will help to instill a sense of trust in communicating with you. That is a rare commodity online!

4. **If you are new online, raise your right hand and repeat after me:**

    - *"I will not forward any dumb joke, 'chain letter,' virus alerts, or unimportant e-mails to my friends without their permission."*
      "I will not forward any dumb joke, 'chain letter,' virus alerts, or unimportant e-mails to my friends without their permission."

    - *"I understand that by doing so, I may fill up their inbox, use other's resources unnecessarily, and may cause other important e-mails to bounce."*

"I understand that by doing so, I may fill up their inbox, use other's resources unnecessarily, and may cause other important e-mails to bounce."

• **"I understand that many onliners have seen those e-mails a million times and find them to be a waste of time."**
"I understand that many onliners have seen those e-mails a million times and find them to be waste of time."

• **"I know that by forwarding so-called humorous e-mails, I may offend people who do not share my sense of humor or annoy those who are sick of having stupid e-mails forwarded to them each time a newbie hops online."**
"I know that by forwarding so-called humorous e-mails, I may offend people who do not share my sense of humor or annoy those who are sick of having stupid e-mails forwarded to them each time a newbie hops online."

• **"I will not take it personally or get upset if some-one asks I not forward unimportant e-mails to them**—especially if I am not including a personal note and just forwarding without comment. *Each person has a right to ask that others not forward jokes, chain letters, or 'forward to your friends' e-mails, and I'll respect that without getting mad."*
"I will not take it personally or get upset if someone asks I not forward unimportant e-mails to them—*especially if I am not including a personal note and just forwarding without comment*. Each person has a right to ask that others not forward jokes, chain letters, or 'forward to your friends' e-mails, and I'll respect that without getting mad."

There! Now, that wasn't too bad, was it? You will no

longer be tempted to forward those jokes or e-mails that instruct you to forward to your friends just because they say so! You will also avoid looking silly and uninformed in the process. Read them if you must, then hit **Delete**. My "Recommend a Dose of Netiquette" at OnlineNetiquette.com is used most often as a way for folks to ask others to please refrain from just forwarding e-mails. If you must forward an e-mail, at the very least, take the time to write a personal note to the person you are forwarding to and include a comment why you think they will be interested. If you cannot come up with something relevant to say, that is a clue to not bother forwarding the e-mail.

Don't ever believe those e-mails that state certain things will happen simply by you forwarding the e-mail to ten friends. Whether it is good luck, money, or health, nothing happens when you forward e-mails of this nature other than wasting other's time and resources! If you don't know for a fact that the e-mail you are forwarding is specifically apropos to the person you are forwarding to and you know they will want to receive it, ask first. One of the most common requests I receive through OnlineNetiquette.com is from onliners wanting to know a "nice way" of telling someone they care about to stop sending hokey, joke, and chain e-mails without hurting their feelings. Speaking for those who know you, we have seen those e-mails before—many are scams, hoaxes, or time wasters—cut us a break!

5. **Never give out phone numbers or personal information** without confirming you are communicating with a reputable party. Ever. Just as in the off-line world, it takes time and consistency to build trust. Don't advise any personal information until you determine you are dealing with a real person who is who they say they are, and even then,

still be very cautious. Don't believe e-mails that state you need to click on a link and provide personal information for any reason—most are scams trying to get information from you to use for identity fraud. For those under the age of eighteen, parental units need to instruct their children that under no circumstances are they to ever divulge their age, location, or any personal information. Parents need to make this one of the house rules of being online, which should also include having the computer in a common area of the house. In addition, no one should ever give out the personal contact information of others without their specific permission to do so.

6. **Always make a reasonable effort to search a Web site for the information you are looking for.** Look for the "Frequently Asked Questions," "Help," or "About Us" sections which exist to give you the answers you seek before you take the site owner's time by e-mailing for information that is readily available on their site. Who would have thought that one day you could log on, search, and find all this information at your fingertips in a matter of moments? It doesn't get any easier than that! To not want to read the available information or resources that have been made accessible to you with such ease is plain old lazy! I get e-mailed daily for answers that are easily found in my Ten Courtesies or in the Internet 101 section of OnlineNetiquette.com if someone were to make minimal effort. I know my site has clear and intuitive navigation—most information being no more than two clicks from my top page. However, I also know that some visitors simply do not want to take the time to read, so they expect me to take the time to repeat what is on my site. I even have a Google Search Toolbar right there to search my site—and they don't even want to take the time to use it by typing in a couple of keywords! Talk about giving the perception of lazy and not respecting other's time!

If a Web site owner takes the time to provide information on their site, read it. No one person's time is more important than another's, and common courtesy includes respecting this fact. If you do not find what you are looking for after making a reasonable effort, search for the appropriate contact area for your question. Do not just click on the first e-mail link you come across and blurt out your question(s). Do not be surprised if your e-mail goes unanswered when the information can be easily found on the site you are e-mailing. And then if you do get a response, don't get mad if the response points you right back to the site. If you cannot find what you are seeking, when you do e-mail for help a nice "thank you for your time" goes a long way to you getting the information you are looking for on a timely basis.

It is also important to keep in mind that the focus of each Web site is up to the site owner—not to the site visitors. Each site cannot be everything to everyone or be what you perceive it should be. Most explain clearly in their Frequently Asked Questions (FAQ) or About Us areas what the specific focus of the site is. So don't e-mail an apple site about where to find oranges! Be sure to review the information provided to double-check that what you seek would even be covered by the site you are at before you e-mail for assistance. And if it isn't, another more refined search will probably produce a site that does.

7. **Do not use Return Receipt Request (RR) for each and every personal e-mail you send** because you like "knowing" when someone opens the e-mail you sent to them. Not only is this an annoyance for the recipient, this feature is intrusive! How would you like it if every time you heard a voicemail, or answering machine message or opened a postal letter, it was immediately reported back to the sender that you had heard or opened their communications? The

recipient should have the privacy to determine when and if they want to review your e-mail and to reply—period. RRs should be reserved for those instances where it is critical to knowing the e-mail was opened. This could include legal and important business issues. Keep in mind that "opened" doesn't necessarily mean "read"!

8. **Understand that you will be on a continual learning curve.** All of us are. I learn something new every day I go into my office—and some ask if I think I am a know-it-all—go figure! The online arena is changing constantly—the only consistency is change! If you do not have the desire to learn and do not make the effort to understand the general rules that apply to the technology in which you are participating, you will not be taken seriously by fellow Netizens. The Internet has always been a self-governing society, and you may receive some pretty terse e-mails from other onliners pointing out your faux pas—some will not be as nice as others. If you do find yourself on the receiving end of such an e-mail, do not fire back at them. If they are right, simply e-mail your "humble apologies" and let them know you will do better as you learn more. You might be surprised when a return e-mail with a much nicer tone shows up in your inbox. Use situations like that as an opportunity to learn what you are doing wrong so you do not continue to upset others.

9. **If you do receive a nasty e-mail, do not respond immediately—if at all.** People are very bold and overly critical on the other side of your computer screen. In my experience, they tend to not hesitate to point out things they think you need improvement on while not even noticing the good or positive points on the very same issue. Most wouldn't talk to you in the same manner if they were face to face with you or even on the telephone. Many times, these onliners are simply trying to get a rise out of

you (this is called trolling) all to make themselves feel self-important. To put it simply—they are just plain jerks. If you do not have something nice to say, or at the very least sternly professional, just hit Delete. If you receive a nasty or hurtful e-mail from someone you care about where obviously there is a misunderstanding (this happens quite often with e-mail), pick up the old-fashioned telephone and talk to them to resolve the situation! Many times, e-mails will only exasperate an already-sticky situation unless both parties are articulate and deliberate communicators.

10. **Keep in mind that all private e-mail is considered to be copyrighted by the original author.** If you post someone's private e-mail to a public list or board or forward it to an outside party in whole or in part, you must include the author's permission to post the material publicly. Not doing so can get you into some deep doo-doo legally or with your friends and associates. Think of it this way . . . how would you feel if a personal, private e-mail that you had written for a specific purpose/person is then plastered across the Internet or forwarded to onliners you do not know? You need to always ask permission before forwarding/posting any private e-mails! If you cannot, will not, or do not have permission, you should never forward private e-mails to others or post them publicly.

11. **Always minimize, compress, or "zip" large files before sending.** Many onliners do not realize how large documents, graphics, or photo files are. Guess what? They are large enough to fill someone's e-mail box and cause their other e-mail to bounce! Get in the habit of reducing the physical size of graphics down to six hundred pixels in width or compressing anything over two hundred thousand bytes just to be safe. If you don't know a file's size, or how to find out its size, learn. Not knowing how is no excuse to slow down or overload someone

else's e-mail inbox! (You can view file sizes in Windows Explorer by simply right clicking on the filename and choosing Properties.) You want to learn how to compress the files or, in the case of graphics, learn how to make them physically smaller with your choice of graphic software. There are several file compression software utilities available online for these purposes.

Rarely does a graphic that you want to share have to be larger than six hundred pixels in width. Or better yet you could be really courteous and learn how to use the free Web space offered by your ISP (Internet Service Provider) to upload photos and simply send the link to friends and family to view. If they want a copy of the photo, all they need to do is right click on it and save a copy to their hard drive. If you do not know how to do any of this, all you have to do is learn! If you haven't noticed, you can literally learn anything online if you just make the effort to look, read, and learn! (Great Resource: HTML Programming and Technology Cheat Sheets: http://www.TechnoChallenged.com.)

It is more convenient for you to just attach files to an e-mail without notice, but it certainly leaves the impression that what you want to do is more important than the other side's inbox limit. Man, is that rude! Did you know that many onliners still have to wait up to thirty minutes or more to download overly large files due to their connection speed? Many who are online not far outside of large metropolitan areas do not have cable or DSL connections; they are on dial-ups—most still only able to connect at 28.8K due to older rural infrastructure.

So with this in mind, do not send unannounced large attachments or multiple attachments to others, especially at night or on weekends when the recipient may not be online to download them, because you think that photo or file is cute or cool or neat. More importantly, when sending attachments for business, always compress them and ask permission first including when would be the best time to send your files. Not doing so will reflect your lack of courtesy for the recipient and your overall lack of technology savvy.

To send large files that take a long time to download that may not respect the other person's time, reflect their sense of humor, point of view, or in the worst case max out their e-mail box is pretty inconsiderate to say the least.

12. Do not forward virus warnings! Forwarding of virus warnings received from friends are generally always hoaxes. The first thing you should do when you receive an e-mail of this type is to visit your virus software provider's Web site. As an example, check out Symantec's Virus Hoax Page:

http://securityresponse.symantec.com/avcenter/hoax.html

In particular, if the e-mail instructs you to forward to everyone you know, or worse yet to remove files from your hard drive, it is a hoax. When you receive e-mails like this, delete them and do not forward them! Definitely ignore those forwarded e-mails instructing you to delete files on your computer—they could be critical files that your computer needs to operate. Your virus software manufacturer's Web site will have detailed solutions on what to do if you have a specific virus. Those are the only instructions you should follow.

Only warn friends if you know for a fact that you have a virus that you have inadvertently passed on to them. Rely only on your virus software and your software provider's

Web site for the real scoop. If you do get one of these wacky e-mails from a friend or associate, you can verify if it is a hoax by going to the Symantec Web site mentioned earlier before you embarrass yourself by forwarding it to everyone you know. Then, I recommend you reply to your friend's e-mail with a link to the page that discusses the hoax, so they are also informed. Simply go to your virus software provider's site and read what they have to say before you unnecessarily alarm your contacts or cause them to delete files off their hard drive, and in the process, you end up looking rather silly, to say the least. All virus providers have hoax pages for this very reason. There are many urban legends purely in existence to watch all the newbies screw up their computer's configuration files or forward to everyone they know and end up looking rather foolish in the process.

a. With the advancement of technology, it is now possible to get a virus without even opening an e-mail. That ended with W32.Nimda.A@mm in September 2001 that merely required you click on the subject of the e-mail in your e-mail program. For those of you that use Outlook as your e-mail program, you are a target if you have your program set to "Preview" e-mail. Preview automatically opens the e-mail for your review, and opening the e-mail could trigger a virus. **HINT: Turn Previewing Off!** Subsequent viruses also propagated by taking advantage of bugs in some servers to plant a virus on the server and then transfer it to those who visit the Web sites on that server. If there is a bug to exploit, it will be exploited! That is why it is so very important to keep your software updated with the latest patches that solve these problems once they are identified.

b. Now it is common for viruses to actually use e-mail addresses collected off your computer, out of your address book or inbox to send the virus and propagate itself to all the addresses found with your name in the **From** field. Some viruses have been known to send out a virus using any e-mail address it finds on your system in the **From** field! Yikes! The need for a 24/7 real-time virus protection software is no longer a choice—it is your responsibility to remain virus free. You also need to update your virus files regularly so that your computer is protected from the latest releases. I recommend you minimally schedule updates daily through the software of your choice or update each time you log on.

c. **Basics for virus protection:**

- Get an active virus protection program that is always *on*. This will catch any viruses as they are being downloaded, so they can be quarantined and cannot infect your system.

- You can only be protected from the latest viruses if your computer knows what to protect you from. Update your virus patterns daily or every time you log on. These updates can be downloaded from the Web site of your virus software manufacturer. Most software packages have a scheduler to tell your computer to do this automatically—how convenient! You need to ensure your system is protected from the latest viruses which may have just been discovered since you were last online. New viruses are identified all the time!

- Never click on any attachment or an .exe file attached within an e-mail without making sure the attachment has been checked for viruses.

Even if the e-mail appears to come from someone you know very well! The person you know unknowingly may be infected and are not aware of the virus on their system; a virus which has just spawned an e-mail that has their name on it and is addressed to you without their knowledge. The e-mail may look like it is from your friend just to get you to open it when in fact it is an e-mail generated by a virus, so it can propagate itself on your computer.

As a courtesy to your fellow Netizens, try to learn what technology is all about—ignorance is not bliss online.

COURTESY NO. 2

PERCEPTION IS THE ONLY
REALITY ONLINE

Always start your e-mail with *Hello, Hi, Dear*, or whatever works for you.

•

One of the primary reasons for writing this book and creating OnlineNetiquette.com was due to my extensive experience with how many onliners do not seem to know or may not care about how they will be perceived. After being online for over ten years, I have determined it could very well be that many do not care because there are tons of resources online to give you the basics if one were to take the time and make the effort to look for them. Too many onliners take no care in the choice of words used, or how the content of their e-mail will reflect on them to the person on the other side. Also, judging by the reaction of some onliners who have been sent to OnlineNetiquette.com, they seem to not want to improve themselves or make the effort to learn the necessary skills to be perceived favorably. Isn't that a shame?

To make claims you have the "right" to say and treat others any way you like further solidifies the reason why there are so many disagreements and unpleasant exchanges online. If you are one of those who do care, one of those who can put your ego on the shelf for a moment and realize we all make mistakes, have more to learn or who up until now may have underestimated the importance of these issues, read on.

When you make a phone call, you always say "hello" to the person who picks up the phone—you don't just start talking about why you are calling or begin asking questions. A little idle chit-chat asking how the other person is, what is new, etc., then entails. I am not suggesting that you have paragraphs of senseless chit-chat in your e-mail before you get to your point, just that you simply show some interest and courtesy to the person on the other side. You may think doing so to be trivial or time wasting; however, this is how a civilized society communicates with one another and how valuable relationships are built. Doing so will also make the recipient look forward to seeing your name in their inbox rather than cringing or jumping for the Delete button. Feel free to use a greeting that reflects your personality and intended level of formality. To just blurt out your comments or questions without a greeting comes off as terse and demanding.

You want to think of your e-mail as a serious communication tool, not an excuse to forget about being professional, courteous, or friendly. To insinuate you are better than others or that your time is too valuable to spend on the formalities mentioned here is to be perceived as not having consideration for the human being on the other end of the pipeline. And that is not cool personally or professionally!

As a courtesy to your fellow Netizens, mind your manners and play nice.

COURTESY NO. 3

PROOFREAD AND CHECK FOR ERRORS

Always spell check your e-mail, proofread for errors, capitalize your sentences, and use appropriate punctuation and grammar.

•

- "If a emale is writon with speeling mestakes and gramitckal errors, you mite git the meening, however, the messige is not as affective, or smoothly redable."

  As the above example proves, poor writing is equivalent to someone speaking with spinach stuck between his/ her teeth. Listeners and readers concentrate on the spinach, not on what is being said.

- Family and friends is one thing. If you feel they do not deserve your effort to make sure they have an easy-to-read e-mail from you, fine—they know you best and are probably the most forgiving. Or they may be one of the many who e-mail me weekly about a way to tell you how you are being perceived without hurting your feelings.

  However, with business acquaintances or other online contacts, proper formatting is crucial to building your relationship and credibility. Don't ever announce to business associates with whom you have become lazy that "I don't spell check or capitalize my sentences with you because we know each other so well." That is simply inconsiderate. By doing so you are basically telling the other person that they are not worth the time it would take for you to communicate properly with them. This will also be a strong indication of your level of education and professionalism. Lack of attention to these details can also open the door for misunderstandings.

- Refrain from using multiple exclamation points (!!!!!) or question marks (?????). Multiple exclamation points and question marks risk giving the impression that you are sarcastic, demanding, and/or condescending. Do you understand??????

You want your e-mails to be readable and offer clarity in meaning. You want to make the effort to type in complete sentences. Create new paragraphs when the subject matter shifts (hit Enter twice). Take the time to review your e-mail before clicking Send. To type random phrases or cryptic thoughts do not lend to clear communication or you being perceived as one who made it out of the sixth grade.

As a courtesy to your fellow Netizens,
communicate clearly and properly
without errors—use the education
you received in grade school.

COURTESY NO. 4

BE SURE TO SIGN OFF

Always end your e-mails with a *Thank you, Sincerely, Take it easy, Best regards—and* your name!

•

- In particular, when you request information or ask something of the one you are e-mailing, have the common courtesy to thank them in advance (TIA!) and sign off your e-mail appropriately. To just click the Send button without even typing your name is impersonal and comes off as overbearing. Not using a proper sign off certainly is not conducive to being perceived as a person one would want to continue to build a relationship or do business with.

- Be sure to always sign your name, handle, nickname, or initial. Use your better judgment as to the level of formality. For example, I use /j, Judi, Judith, or Judith Kallos depending on whom I am communicating with and the level of formality desired. Not doing so comes off as demanding or presumptuous. If you don't want to type your name every time, then incorporate it into your signature file in your e-mail program that is automatically appended to the end of every e-mail.

- Never just forward an e-mail without a comment as to why you are forwarding the e-mail to the intended party. To do so is assuming and lazy. Do you want the party to comment or review? Is there a specific issue you want them to address? Did you have a particular reason why you forwarded that particular e-mail to them? Always let the recipient know why you are forwarding an e-mail to them. Including what, if anything, you need them to respond to or what action is required by them.

- If you are e-mailing for support, asking a question, or requesting assistance from the person you are e-mailing, it would behoove you to say "thank you." It is very easy to come off as bossy in e-mail—people do not take warmly to those who are bossy.

  By sending an e-mail that blurts out a question or demands a response without even closing with "appreciate your help" or "thank you in advance" or even "let me know what you think" you can bet the person on the other side will not respond as quickly, work as hard, take you as seriously, or possibly not even care to respond at all. Know this to be a fact. When the other side does respond and take the time to help you, take a moment and send a quick reply e-mail thanking them for their assistance. This only takes a moment and will be greatly appreciated by the person on the other side who you can bet is getting more e-mails that are rude and demanding than courteous.

- As a general rule of thumb, if someone takes the time to e-mail you and it is not junk mail or offensive, give them the courtesy of a return response in a timely manner. By not doing so, you appear to ignore them.

How would you feel if the e-mail you sent was simply ignored? A short and sweet acknowledgment of their e-mail commenting on the issues within only takes a moment.

As a courtesy to your fellow Netizens,
be polite and type to those as you would
have them type unto you.

COURTESY NO. 5

INSTANT MESSAGING TIPS

**Use instant messaging (IM) properly with
consideration for the person on the other side.**

•

Many of the issues that apply to e-mail apply to instant messaging and vice versa. The key once again is courtesy and clarity in your communications.

- Start by always asking if the person you are IMing is available and if it is a good time to chat. I get e-mail all the time from onliners who get frustrated by others thinking they should be available 24/7 or whenever they are online. If they are busy, ask them when they will be free. You do the same—if you are busy and cannot chat, let the other person know and advise when you can connect at a later time.

- Practice communicating briefly and succinctly. Clarity is even more important when you are IMing. IM is meant for brief communications—not your manifesto on the day's events. If the topic is that long winded or complicated, ask when would be a good time to give them a call on the telephone to discuss the topic further.

- Use IM for casual topics or informational briefs. Serious topics are not conducive to IM. Certain topics and situations require face-to-face meetings or at the very least a telephone call or card stating your feelings. IM is not the place for serious topics or confrontational issues where emotions are involved.

- As I mentioned in previous courtesies, IMing is not an excuse to forget your grade-school education. Check your spelling and grammar as best you can within this environment. IM is a communications tool nonetheless. If you must use acronyms, be sure to only use those acronyms that are commonly known or understood to maintain the clarity of your comment.

- If you are not an accomplished multitasker (and most folks are not), don't continue multiple IM sessions and leave onliners hanging while you communicate with others. The majority of onliners are simply not good enough multitaskers to offer each person their full attention while IMing different topics with different contacts. Do not leave others hanging while you try and hold a conversation with more than one person. Not only is doing so perceived as discourteous, you are not giving the other person your full attention and thereby wasting their time. This can give them the impression you do not feel their time is valuable.

- Learn how to use the features of your IM program. Specifically, become familiar with your "busy" and "away" message features. Using these features will make it easier for those trying to communicate with you to know your status and avoid miscommunications about your availability. For those that don't take your "busy" and "away" messages seriously, or do not respect your time when you are online, it is time to use the "ignore" feature. The Ignore button is a built-in feature that will allow you to block communications from anyone you choose. You can allow only certain people to contact you or block certain users from contacting you at all. Use your "ignore" feature sparingly for those who do not respect your time or your requests for contact at a later time.

- Never IM under an alias to take a peak at friends' or associates' activities—how rude!

- Take into consideration whom you are communicating with to determine the acronyms and emoticons that should be used—if at all. Certainly you wouldn't use the same with a business associate versus your mom who may not even know what the acronyms and emoticons mean. Use your common sense here!

- **Word of Caution:** As with e-mail, IMs can be saved and sent to others. Once you send it, it is gone. If you are upset, sign off until you cool off. Don't type what you wouldn't want to be passed around. I get e-mails all the time from IMers who are upset because they sent a private note to a friend they thought they could trust who then broadcasted their IM across the Net. Know whom you can trust, and only trust those you know!

- **A Word to Business Onliners:** Be professional even though IM tends to be a more informal environment. When it comes to business, everything you do and how you choose to do it will reflect on you and contribute to how you are perceived. Keep in mind the quality and tone of your messages reflect on your overall level of professionalism. A spelling and grammar check is imperative in any form of business communications regardless of mode used. As mentioned earlier, I've found that most people are unable to multitask successfully—be realistic about your skills in this area and do not overestimate your abilities. Making associates wait while communicating with other business associates could cause lost opportunity. It could affect your business, a promotion, a contact, or worse yet, your job. If you are having multiple IM exchanges at a single time, better to limit yourself and communicate the right message—than to confuse messages or tone between IMers. As a courtesy, even more so for business communications, if you are unable to respond because of a deadline or a meeting, set yourself to "busy," so your colleagues will know that you are unable to respond and are not just ignoring them.

As a courtesy to your fellow Netizens, communicate with clarity while learning how to use your software appropriately.

COURTESY NO. 6

RESPOND PROMPTLY AND DOWN EDIT

**When replying to e-mails, always respond promptly
and edit out any unnecessary information
from the post you are responding to.**

•

- Responding promptly is simply the courteous thing to do. Don't leave those who have taken the time to contact you wonder if you received the e-mail or are ever going to respond to their communications. Think about how quickly you would return a phone call or voice mail. E-mail is no different especially considering most onliners have expectations of a faster response as e-mail is sent and usually received so quickly. Outside of any emergencies such as surgery or lack of connectivity, always respond as soon as you can. If you need more time to gather your thoughts, simply pop off an e-mail stating you did receive the e-mail and that you are planning on responding in more detail and when.

- Don't just hit the Reply button and start typing. Edit out (down edit) unimportant parts of the e-mail you are responding to and respond point by point. Yes, there may be times where keeping in the entire previous e-mail is important, especially if you are adding onliners to the conversation via **CC**. But that is the rare occasion—here again, use your common sense.

Editing your e-mail is accomplished by deleting information from the previous mail that is not necessary to continuing the conversation. At the very least, edit out e-mail headers and signature lines. Lazy is hitting Reply and sending a one-word answer . . . please. Always respond with proper sentence structure and a full explanation. Is your time really more important than those you are corresponding with that you cannot respond properly and make the other side possibly wonder what you mean? Aren't your associates or friends worth taking the time to make communicating with you a pleasant experience because they always understand what you mean?

More importantly when e-mail conversations on the same topic are ongoing, down editing is critical to keeping the conversation on track. Why would you possibly want to have copies of the last three to four (or more) e-mails added to the growing list of back-and-forth? You make the person you are communicating with look to see if you may have included a response amongst all the previous text or even wonder what you may be specifically replying to. If you just respond on the top of the message, delete all the previous back-and-forths before the very last that you are responding to. When you are ready to respond to a point within an e-mail, put your cursor after what you are going to comment on, and be sure to hit the Enter key twice before typing. This ensures that your comments do not blend with the previous text that you are responding to.

By not editing your e-mail, your lack of understanding in regard to smooth communications, bandwidth, and trying to keep the online environment not overloaded with unnecessary noise will be apparent. Always edit/ delete what is not necessary for the conversation to continue. This is a skill well worth developing that over time can add tremendous clarity to your communications both personally and professionally. If you are not clear how to do so, you can always e-mail me so you can see how I reply.

Editing your e-mail is a skill that is developed over time by doing. Everyone edits in their own sort of unique way depending on their personality and the points they want to focus on and address. Here are some quick tips to help you on your way.

- Once you hit Reply, you can remove any part of the e-mail that is not necessary to the clarity of the ongoing conversation. This includes e-mail headers and closing signature lines. Never just hit Reply and start typing, leaving all the previous e-mail(s) in place. Of course there will be situations where you want to ensure a record of the conversation is in place and keep all of the previous e-mail(s) intact, but that is generally not the case in day-to-day communications.

- The best way to edit properly is to hold your left mouse button down and drag it over the text you want removed then hit Delete. Hit your Enter key twice to put a line space between the content above, and then start typing your comments related to that particular section. Then continue to do the same as the e-mail continues. Remove what doesn't matter, leave what does; hit Enter twice, and type your reply.

- When removing a big chunk of the e-mail, you can let the person you are responding to know that, yes, you did read that section but have no comment by including <snip> where your editing stopped and the comments you will be replying to begin. Most times, a comment is not necessary to every word in an e-mail sent to you. This way, folks know you are not ignoring anything, just that you have nothing to say at that moment and "snipped" that portion of the e-mail.

- E-mails become more difficult to follow when you start adding up all the >>>>s. It is a good idea to get in the habit of starting a new e-mail after three > are in the return. At that point, most likely updating the **Subject** field of your e-mail to better reflect the current direction of the conversation will be in order as well. If the subject of the conversation has changed, always change the **Subject** field. You can type in the new subject in the **Subject** field right before the original subject and still include the original subject by putting **was:** in front of the original subject that has now been changed. These extra efforts help avoid misunderstandings due to all the back-and-forths.

Integrating these simple steps when replying to e-mail can help keep your conversations on track and easier for all to read. Besides, by setting a good example, others can learn from you—and that is a good thing!

As a courtesy to your fellow Netizens,
respond promptly, and please down edit your
posts keeping only what will contribute
to the ongoing conversation.

COURTESY NO. 7

THOU SHALL NOT SPAM

Never, ever, ever; never send anyone a commercial e-mail about your product or service if the recipient did not specifically e-mail you for that information and you are responding to their request.

•

Contrary to those who argue this point with me when I ask them to cease spamming my e-mail addresses or those of my clients, sending Unsolicited Commercial E-mail (UCE) is not an accepted practice of cold calling or lead generating.

un·so·lic·it·ed: Not looked for or requested; unsought

As a matter of fact, many states and the U.S. government have or are considering legislation for these types of activities. In addition, the new U.S. anti-spam law requires as of January 1, 2004, that all commercial e-mail communications include a physical address. Don't be misled to think that because spammers include a physical address that makes spamming OK as many of these e-mails now state—that is not the case.

The way online works is you should have a great-looking Web site that gets found when looked for. That is just one of many ways to generate leads online. E-mailing strangers is not one of them. Worse yet, to do so and include an attachment not only shows your lack of respect for those you are e-mailing, but your complete lack of understanding in regard to the very technology you are using! Your actions will most certainly have a negative effect on how you are perceived, not to mention greatly minimizing your future business potential.

Common courtesies go a long way online when trying to foster relationships of any kind—including the perception that you understand how to correctly use technology. Including an overly large attachment that is not compressed in a format that requires one have the same software as you do (don't count on the fact they do) will cause those on the other side to wonder what else you don't get. If you send a WordPerfect document, the other side needs to also have WordPerfect to view that document. Why would someone want to do business with you when you make it unnecessarily difficult due to your lack of understanding? Files should only be sent in a format that you know the other side has the appropriate software to view—because you asked first! No, not everyone has MS Publisher or PowerPoint.

To assume that what you determine to be informative or useful will be accepted in kind by people you may not know very well, or at all for that matter, is a poor assumption at best. To assume that onliners "need" the information you want to provide as though if given a choice they wouldn't know better and you need to send it anyway is condescending in tone. These actions can produce dramatic reactions from those sick and tired of being sent information, files, or attachments they did not request and wouldn't request if given the opportunity. This includes not only commercial sales collateral or spam but for the "send to all your friends" e-mails that many who have been online for sometime now have filtered directly to our trash.

As mentioned earlier, do not forward "informative" e-mails that say "forward to everyone you know." In fact if the e-mail says that, you're safe to just hit Delete. Dime to a dollar "everyone" will not appreciate your efforts. No, it does not matter how nice or commendable the topic supposedly is or your personal views consider it to be.

- To assume that because so many people are sending junk e-mail that means it is "OK," acceptable, or the same as cold-calling off-line, you couldn't be further from the truth. Cold-calling online is called spam! Spammers get their accounts cancelled by ISPs every day. Credible, ethical business onliners simply do not e-mail potential business contacts or customers they do not know about their commercial enterprise, services, or products *without permission first*. Especially when including files that are large and software specific.

- This includes going from Web site to Web site and pasting your generic sales pitch into their online form. You are still sending unsolicited commercial e-mail to someone who didn't ask for it. Using a Web site's contact form to get your information in someone's inbox does not negate that fact. Unless your promotional e-mail specifically has a product or service that the Web site you are contacting would be interested in because it applies to the topic or focus of the site don't proceed. The best way to sell to other sites through their contact form is to ask first! Send a short e-mail asking if they would be interested in your product or service and if you can send additional information their way. If you do not get a response, that means no!

- There is no government law or statue that now authorizes unsolicited e-mail as many spammers state at the end of their junk mail. If you believe these comments, you are the type of onliner these spammers are counting on! Remember, online, one can type anything they please—that does not make their claims ethical, true, or accurate. There are no remove lists when it comes to spammers or companies you have not had previous contact with. **Never follow instructions** from unscrupulous spammers that state you just need to hit Reply to be removed from further mailings. That is an outright fib and a way to track valid e-mail addresses for future mailings. If you do hit Reply to unsubscribe, most likely you will have just confirmed you are a "live" account and your junk mail will increase exponentially as your e-mail address is resold over and over again.

- Those who spam (send junk e-mail) are looked at as intrusive, lazy, obnoxious, unethical, and unable to make a buck the right way—by working hard, by doing their due diligence, by having a credible product or needed service that one can view at their nice-looking Web site that gets found when looked for. Run from the business that when you point out their spam is not appreciated they flame you back with name-calling and accusations that *you* don't get it. These are the worst onliners of all, and they deserve to be reported to their ISP or hosting company which will weed through the e-mail to determine where it really originated and report them if at all possible.

- Have you noticed how most spammers do **not** have a Web site (or if they do it is the epitome of amateurish) and/or they hide their e-mail identity? Why do you think that is if spamming is OK as they would like you to believe?

  1. Because they would be reported to their Web site hosting company and most likely their Web site, if they even have one, will be shut down.

2. Their ISP will cancel their account upon receipt
    of spam complaints or ensuing mail bombs that
    slow down their network. A mail bomb is when
    a particular e-mail address is sent thousands
    and thousands of e-mails an hour to overload
    the system.

3. Their Web site or company name would end up
    on the many blacklist sites run by people on a
    mission to portray spammers for what they are.
    Snake oil salesmen!

If you are not sure how to market your product or service
online within established guidelines, hire a professional
to help you out, so you have the best chance for
success and to help keep you out of trouble.

When it comes to spam, just remember what your
mother used to say, "If everyone jumped off a bridge,
would you?"

As a courtesy to your fellow Netizens,
don't fill their inboxes with e-mail only you
feel is important without their permission first.

COURTESY NO. 8

YOU ARE WHAT YOU WRITE

How you communicate, the words you choose and how you choose to use them will give a clear indication as to the kind of person you are. Learn to write with clarity, and take onliners at their word—not what you "think" they mean.

•

It should go without saying that sending e-mail with extremely foul, threatening, or abusive language is not acceptable in any form of communications. This includes obscenities, verbal harassment, threats of slander, or personal comments that would prove offensive based on race, religion, or sexual orientation. Unfortunately, I see these type of communications all too often across the Web.

- No matter how rude someone may be to you, or how offended you may be by another's opinion, don't lower yourself to their level by stooping to obscenities or threats and claims of self-importance. Stick to the facts at hand and try not to take comments personally or make the discussion "about you." Always state your opinion clearly and concisely, without personalizing an issue or resorting to name-calling. Be careful to not read anything into an e-mail that isn't there. Take onliners at their word, and in the same vein, if you type it, you'd better mean it! That is why it is so important to follow the guidelines in this book and to choose your words very carefully. There are many heated discussions online. There are just as many e-mails that are sent without enough thought being given to tone or perceived intent. Hold your head high and communicate as an adult, share your opinions and point of view, and realize that in the grand scheme of things for the most part nobody is "better" than anybody else by virtue of their opinions alone. Sometimes it is just best to not reply at all.

- If you have mistakenly offended or have misinterpreted what another person wrote, please do not hesitate to apologize. Apologizing is something not practiced as often as it should. Isn't anyone wrong anymore? That being said, "apologies" which are only offered to produce an opportunity to continue a tirade from a previous e-mail are viewed as self-righteous. Apologies should only be offered with sincerity. Certainly, this does not mean you need to apologize to everyone who has a different or overly critical opinion than you do. We are all individuals, and the majority of us are good people who do our best to do the right thing. No one person is authorized to be the one who is always right or the only one whose opinion counts. There are many of these types of onliners who will take the time to point out negatives without taking notice or mentioning any of the positives. More often than not, these personalities end up being viewed as arrogant and assuming.

Know you have done your best and take constructive criticism in stride. None of us is perfect—nor do I think we would want that responsibility! If you make a mistake, make note and put the appropriate corrections or modifications in place to prevent the same from happening in the future.

- This is a good time to keep in mind that you never put anything in an e-mail that you don't want the world to know about. E-mails get reported and forwarded to public newsgroups and message boards and can be produced at a later date. Personal e-mails should not be forwarded without permission; however, you can count on the fact that it happens anyway. Always be better than a disagreeable communicator and "agree to disagree" like most adults do. Don't get bold just because you feel you are safely behind your computer screen and make statements that are untruths. If you would not reply to someone the very same way if you were there in person with them, you probably should not reply at all. By not replying in kind, you hold yourself to a higher standard and leave the other party left to look like the fool they just made of themselves. Make an effort to always take the high ground.

- Due to the lack of vocal and nonverbal clues with e-mail, we often forget that eye contact, tone of voice, and body language, which we take for granted when communicating in person, are not available in online communications. Use emoticons and acronyms when necessary to convey your message and set the tone. If you are joking, include a smiley face :-); if you are sad or upset, you can use :-(. If you are unsure of someone's intent or meaning, ask them before making accusations that you may regret. Don't assume what anyone means—take them at their word(s)—same as you should expect to be responsible for every word that you type. I have a list of the most popular emoticons later in this book that gives you a plethora of choices, so you can communicate your emotions to avoid miscommunications. When you send out an e-mail, the recipient will be hanging on every word and each word's specific meaning. "I didn't mean it that way" does not apply online. If you type it, expect the recipient will assume you meant it.

Check out the emoticons and acronyms chapter for lists of the most used symbols.

- Keep in mind when in newsgroups or on message boards that you are in a global arena. There are charters and rules you need to make yourself aware of. To post without making this effort could induce responses from seasoned Netizens pointing you to sites such as OnlineNetiquette.com or, believe it or not, much worse. There will be those reading your posts in countries from around the world that may not have the same religious or social views that you have by virtue of their culture. They also may not have a firm understanding of the English language. Do your best to keep this in mind.

As a courtesy to your fellow Netizens,
please choose your words carefully
and refrain from abusive or threatening
behavior and language.

COURTESY NO. 9

SAY NO TO TROLLS

Don't fall for flamers, jerks, or "trolls."

•

"Trolling" is the practice of sending or posting obviously offensive comments, brutally untruthful statements or words and phrases that we all know to be those that would instigate a fight if stated in the local tavern.

When you see posts or receive e-mail that is so obviously offensive or rude, you can bet that someone is trying to "get your goat" and is basically a jerk. This is a common practice in newsgroups and on discussion boards and forums. You have some online knucklehead with too much time and too little of a life who posts to a group something they know to be very inflammatory. They can rely on the fact that at the very least the newbies will not recognize they are "trolling" and will not be able to ignore their post. The newbies then flame back with venom and vigor. The instigating troller then sits back and watches the thread (conversation) continue, knowing they did it just to get a reaction . . . and it worked! A full-fledged flame war of nasty e-mails begins to grow back and forth until the administrator is then forced to end the thread and take it off the table.

In these situations where posts to a group are so obviously inflammatory and you begin to see others start chiming in, you are then witnessing the start of a flame war. Nothing positive or constructive ever comes from this type of situation. It is best you do not become involved thereby contributing to an unproductive discussion. Pass up any urge to communicate with those that do not have the same moral and ethical behavior as you do. Report them to the administrator in case the administrator is not aware of the post so that member and post can be immediately removed. If you just know you will not be able to communicate with clarity based on an exchange of ideas without degrading to name-calling and personal insults, click away, leave, find other like minds to spend your time with. It is not your mission in life to show them the light or try to change their opinion. Sometimes it is best to just walk away when conversations degrade and mature conversations based in reality are no longer possible. With Netizens like this, keep in mind their only goal is to annoy you no matter what your opinion is. There are those out there where you just can't win. So just move on and find others with like interests to communicate with.

This is not to say you should not respond to any e-mail that may have a different opinion to yours or negative content. Healthy, constructive conversations and debates are one of the neat parts of being online that gives us exposure to new ideas or different points of view. The unfortunate part is that some onliners don't realize when they are wrong, have been rude, or are not playing by the rules. Part of participating online is that there will be times that you will get e-mail from others who may not be happy with something you said, who may have a difference of opinion, or who are simply misinformed.

Calmly and professionally respond to their e-mail point by point. Even though their opinion is just that—their opinion—they may not have all the facts or are unwilling to look at themselves constructively because you hit a soft spot. Nothing you can do about that other than to e-mail back with your comments and hold the high ground. Don't lower yourself to their level by resorting to the very same ambiguous accusations or personal digs that have nothing to do with the issues in dispute. If your reply produces even more of the same from the sender, don't reply again. It is clear there is nothing you can say to appease this type of individual who more times than not is overly bold because they have the ability to hide behind their computer screen. At that point, it is recommended that you simply create a filter in your e-mail program to identify their e-mail address on the download and send it directly to your trash.

If unfortunately, you do get harassed or threatened, do not hesitate to send a copy of the offending e-mail in its entirety to the sender's ISP. This does not include those who simply have a different opinion than yours and state so clearly without using obscenities or resorting to personal name-calling or threats. Report ongoing threatening or abusive e-mail of this nature to the offender's ISP by sending an e-mail to: abuse@theirISPhere.com. Abuse@ is the general e-mail address most connectivity providers and ISPs accept e-mail complaints through. Always double-check your provider's Web site for details on reporting abusive e-mails.

If their e-mail address is the "dot-com" to their Web site, you need to determine where their dot-com is hosted to send your complaint to the appropriate party which is the hosting company storing the domain and their Web site. You can check where domains are hosted at most any domain registrar using their search feature. Search for a domain, then look for the listing of the DNS servers which are usually near the bottom of the domain name record and that will tell you where you can lodge your complaint.

As a courtesy to your fellow Netizens, don't contribute to a troller's bait or a flame war. There are many more productive and enjoyable things to do online.

COURTESY NO. 10

THE HUMAN TOUCH

Share information and help other newbies online.

•

One of the most disheartening things about technology is that many times people have forgotten the human touch. There are living, breathing human beings at these keyboards. Some onliners are more able to communicate clearly than others based on level of education or level of exposure to technology.

Share your online information and experience with those you know to be new to the online arena. Send them to OnlineNetiquette.com, give them this book, and teach them what you have learned—possibly the hard way—so they will not make the same mistakes as you did. Be open and willing to keep on learning and improving your skills. Don't let your pride stop you from understanding the importance of the issues relayed in this book, by letting your ego get in the way and blur your common sense with anger or feeling as though you have been insulted. If you were given this book as a gift or as part of an assignment or presentation, take a deep breath and do not blame the person who did you the courtesy. Actually you should thank them for turning you on to this very important information! Just because you may not like what you are reading here or how I may present it doesn't make it any less important or relevant to how you will be perceived in your use of technology.

Just as in the off-line world, there is what is called socially acceptable behavior and common courtesy that applies to the online world as well. Do not for a moment think that because you are safely behind a monitor that gives you the excuse to be lazy, rude, crude, obnoxious, or just a plain jerk. You need to be aware of and practice the information in this book if you want to be perceived favorably. Even more so if you are online for commercial gain. To think you don't have to abide by this information or that you can do what you want will be an error in judgment you will soon regret.

Learn to communicate your thoughts and ideas clearly using the accepted practices included in this book. To not do so does us all an injustice. If your writing skills are anemic, stop by your local bookstore or an online bookseller and purchase a book to guide you. Do not let this wonderful communication tool turn into one that is used as an excuse to not learn and use the skills of the written word we all should have learned in school or to not treat others as you would have them treat you. If one is ignorant, it is because they have chosen to be ignorant—make the choice to reverse that pattern and learn, learn, learn.

If you choose to do otherwise, you will be thought of in the most undesirable terms—whether you agree—like it or not.

*As a courtesy to your fellow Netizens,
act like a human being and make an effort
to understand the arena in which you
are participating and then share
your experience with others.*

ARE YOU A TECHNOLOGY MUSHROOM?

You know what they say about mushrooms? Kept in the dark, fertilized with—well, you know.

fungus (n):

> a parasitic plant lacking chlorophyll, leaves, true stems, roots and reproducing by spores

Yuck! Then, what the heck is a *technology mushroom*? I meet, speak, and e-mail with them on a regular basis. Technology mushrooms are those human beings frustrated with technology (Who isn't on occasion?) who really believe that by remaining in the dark, online knowledge, benefits, and success will happen anyway. How? By osmosis? Where they got that idea other than from their own wishful thinking or the spam in their inbox is beyond me. While in that dark corner they believe they will still have fun online, make new friends and acquaintances, opportunities will arise, contacts will be solidified, and leads will be generated. You can tell the "shrooms" as they are the ones who don't make much effort to learn the rules of the online road or even the basics of e-mail. They are typically the first to scream "I'm not a techie, and I don't want to deal with this!" Does this sound like you?

Well, if you are just online for fun or e-mail as part of your job, or you want to have your own Web site someday, you'd better get resolved to the fact that it will behoove you to become as much of a "techie" as you can stand. It really cannot be avoided. You cannot succeed in the dark. Why would one proclaim they don't want to be a "techie" as they proceed to participate in *techie*-nology? Are we so spoiled that we don't want to learn or work at anything and really believe good things will just "happen" purely "because"? Or worse yet, that we can do what we want regardless of how that affects others online? Neither is the case.

I've been involved in the tech scene for decades; the online world since the late '80s. To this day, I learn something new every day, embrace the challenges around every corner, get excited by the unbelievable potential and opportunity technology offers each of us, both for personal improvement and professional development. That is if we want it and want to put the appropriate efforts in the right areas to do things right. Unfortunately, many prefer to remain mushrooms and actually put what little effort they are willing to contribute to their technology experience into complaining and ensuring they remain in the dark.

Technology is a learning experience on a daily basis for all of us—no matter how long you have been involved. The challenges and learning curve will never end. I believe that technology has moved beyond most folk's comprehension and the average person's ability to embrace it—without heavy doses of frustration. You know that saying that goes something like "anything worth having isn't easy"? That's technology! In the long run, however, when it comes to technology the benefits far outweigh the frustration.

So since I get snapped at daily by a shroom or two, I thought I would give you some tips to help you relieve that frustration, put things in perspective, and let you know what you need to prepare for as well as making sure you have realistic expectations. You'll have a lot more fun with technology by choosing to not be a shroom—really! No, I don't expect to turn you into a techie overnight. But I can certainly help you come out of the dark and into the sun, and maybe, just maybe, you may bloom into a dandelion. Dandelions use the sun and grow and prosper. Put weed killer on them, they come back. Pull them out, they come back. Lack of rain, they still grow! Forget the shroom mentality—online you need to think like a dandelion!

- **Cut yourself some slack:** There is no way you will ever get a handle on and know how to do everything that has to do with technology. Make a list of the issues you want to address, the things you want to learn. List them in an order of priority that matches your goals—personally or professionally. Then tackle one issue at a time and master it. Stick to a timetable to complete your list in a realistic time frame and don't put this off! Mastering your new online skills will require tremendous personal discipline because regardless of what all the junk mail would like you to believe, only you can make things happen.

- **Make the time:** Time is not infinite. As we all too often realize much too late, there isn't an abundant supply of time. Only so much in a day as they say. So look at your schedule and see where you can slip in an hour here or fifteen minutes there to dedicate to your quest for online knowledge and skill acquisition. Once again, make the personal commitment to stick to that schedule! Making time when you are booked solid with other responsibilities requires your commitment to stick to that schedule, or it will never happen. You won't learn the things you will need to be successful and enjoy technology unless you do. It won't happen by osmosis!

- **Find your guru:** I've been called a guru on many occasions. But what I really am is someone who has been involved since the beginning, totally Type A who loves the challenges technology offers up on a daily basis. You need to find someone you can rely on to give you the straight scoop—the reality of the online world. You do want the truth, right? Yes, it may seem that everyone is an "expert," however, most of these "experts" only know just a tad more than you do! Your guru could be a friend, a neighbor, or a consultant you found through networking. When you find your guru who has a proven successful online track record, trust them, listen to them, and follow their recommendations. Don't challenge them because you are frustrated or second-guess them based on some spam that landed in your inbox. If you disregard their recommendations or get mad at them when they say things you may not want to hear about what is truly required to participate in the online environment, they may not want to continue to offer their valuable time to you. You must have an attitude that will allow you to have an open mind to new ideas and concepts so that you can learn.

From a business point of view, successful gurus have word-of-mouth referrals sending them more clients than they know what to do with. Even though you are the "customer" or a good friend, the truth is that you need their knowledge, expertise, and experience more than they need you. As with any relationship, treat anyone who is helping you out—whether you are paying or not—with respect, and you will always get more than you pay for. Treat them poorly or pull the "customer is always right" attitude, when in fact you are most likely uninformed, and they may choose to not work with you, and you will have lost a valuable partner. Online, the partners you have on your side can literally make the difference between your failure or success! If they are a true guru, let them guru you! Don't get upset or take it personally if they disagree with some misinformation you confront them with that you "heard from a friend," or if they challenge you to be the best you can be, so you can succeed. The worst thing you can do is gravitate toward those who make technology sound easy—it simply isn't. As a matter of fact, run in the opposite direction of anyone who tries to feed you those spores!

- **Learn your tools:** First and foremost, you need to have a strong understanding about how to use your main technology tool—your computer! Take a class, read a book, rely on resources to teach you how your computer works from directory structure to copying and pasting. In addition, there are three pieces of software that based on your ability to use them correctly and efficiently will make a humongous difference in your level of frustration and ability to use technology properly. Your e-mail program, your virus software, and your Web browser. Make the time to take the tutorials each offers either in the Help menu or at the software manufacturer's site. Master their options and functionality, because when used properly these tools can be a partner in your enjoyment of the online world and your success! Check out my site which offers cheat sheets that give you tips to learn in a nice, easy, and condensed manner: BuyTechieStuff.com. Use promo code—bnmbook—and get a 10 percent discount!

- **Understand the culture:** There are protocols and "rules" that have been in existence on the Internet since before the World Wide Web. The Internet, contrary to popular belief, is not a free-for-all. Read up and learn, then practice the guidelines required for participation. After you read this book, keep it on hand for future reference. Already you're off to a running start! Don't think because the lack of an off-line formal law makes it OK for you to just disregard the established ways of communicating online.

- **E-mail skills are mandatory:** As I've repeated in this book, you will be perceived by your e-mail and writing skills. Don't build these skills, and your communications and success level will suffer or be nonexistent. Understand that others do not have anything other than your e-mail to judge you by. As in the off-line world, there is no friendly face, warm handshake, or eye contact that helps to build trust in the online environment. Only your words and how you choose to use them will be a window into the type of person you are. I've met many a great off-line salesperson that cannot put two sentences together in writing—no matter how great their skills are off-line, without e-mail skills the very same salesperson will fail miserably online. Underestimate how your e-mail will portray you at your own risk!

- **Set realistic goals:** No, you don't have to have an inch-thick business plan reflecting where every moment and penny will be spent for the next five years. But . . . it would be a darned good idea to have some sort of written plan. Fail to plan; plan to fail. I recommend to all those I work with to get a notebook that they call their Web Book. Carry it around with you always. Then if you get an idea or think of something you want to learn, you can write it down before you forget it. You won't remember it later—believe me! I have a ton of great ideas I just know are swimming around in my head that I didn't take the time to write down. Use the list analogy and write down what you want to accomplish and when, in order of priority. Review your list regularly to make sure you are on track. Maybe only schedule to learn something new once each week if that minimizes your frustration. If you miss a date, don't beat yourself up. Reschedule that goal for next week and make sure it happens!

- **Accept change and more change:** Technology is

rocking and rolling! Professionals who live this gig ten to twelve hours every day have a hard time keeping up with the latest information, trends, new products, and opportunities. So be prepared to roll with those proverbial punches. Realize that by becoming involved in technology, you are getting involved in an arena that is in constant flux. This will not change for the foreseeable future, so do not get frustrated when you find you are having difficulty absorbing all the new information that becomes available. Take things in small chunks!

It is not the strongest of the species that survive nor the most intelligent, but those most adaptive to change.

—Charles Darwin

■ **Pay attention to details:** You need to pay attention to every detail involved in your online activities. Lack of attention to detail, whether it be typos, incorrect information, poor timing or planning will be the kiss of death. Technology is nothing if not a gigantic bushel of details that you need to review, change, and address regularly. Everyone is human, and we all will make mistakes. No big deal as long as the mistakes are addressed rather than ignored. If you don't pay attention to all the details in your online communications or in running your online program, your online program won't pay much attention to you. When it comes to other's mistakes, point them out in a kind and helpful manner and remember no one makes mistakes intentionally.

And last but certainly not least . . .

■ **Patience is a virtue:** And a necessity online. As with any new endeavor or venture off-line, online success takes patience, tenacity, and dedication to learn the skills and acquire the knowledge necessary to enjoying and benefiting from this arena. Technology will push you to the edge; your patience will be tried at levels you would never have imagined possible. Patience with your friends, family, business partners, employees, and customers will ensure the health of your business and online relationships for the long term. In the online world, remember that you will need to rely on many friends, associates, and professionals to help you succeed—some of them starting as only friends and turning into partners in your success.

So come out of the dark and into the light! Online opportunities abound for personal and professional growth, and they are there for the taking. But not for everyone . . . "everyone" doesn't have the desire and commitment required to embrace the online environment. It won't happen without *you!*

THE SCOOP ON FILES

Part of being online is learning certain basics so that you are not only informed and perceived as an individual who understands the technology in which you are participating but to also ensure those you communicate with have a pleasant and easy experience. We are going to cover the basics of how to name and organize your files including sending them via e-mail. Not knowing these basics, and understand these are the basics, could cause you lost opportunity with potential contacts or customers that are aware of and practice these basic skills.

LEARN HOW TO NAME FILES PROPERLY

•

There are several basics when naming files that you should make an effort to follow. This is important in keeping files cross platform and so that when they arrive on the other side the intended recipient has the best chance to open them. Let's cover some of the naming conventions.

LENGTH OF FILENAMES

•

Many programs allow you to use long filenames and eliminate file extensions from your view. That doesn't mean that long filenames are OK in all situations or that the ending extensions (*.doc*, *.jpg*, *.gif*, etc.) are not necessary. For the best results, try and stick to what is called the 8.3 pattern. Remember that MS DOS, which requires an 8.3 pattern, still lurks in many computer systems, including many Windows (PC) systems. By an "8.3 pattern," I mean eight letters in the filename followed by the three-letter file extension such as .wks, .pdf, .wps, etc. Extensions are needed for browsers and programs to "recognize" a file and startup the proper program or utility that can read it. Some examples of file extensions are: .doc, .wps, .gif, .txt, .jpg, .rtf, .tif, .ppt, .pdf.

If the files are going to be used on your Web site, the filenames become part of the page's URL or the code to display the file so "picutureofmykidsfifteenthbirthdayboy wasitfun.jpg" is simply not a good idea. When it comes to filenames, shorter is better! A better example: johns15.jpg. Don't name files with sentence-long names. Keep filenames as short and sweet as possible.

NAMING FILES

•

As mentioned above, using an 8.3 pattern is a good safety measure to follow anytime you are naming computer files, more so if they will be used on the Web. Even though you may be able to use a longer filename on your computer, I recommend getting used to and using the 8.3 convention (eight or less character name with a three-character exten-sion, such as "yourpage.doc" or "your_graphic.jpg"). Yes, you can use longer names, and in certain situations even online that is not a problem. However, as a courtesy to those you are sending to, keep it short and sweet—no more than ten to fifteen characters if you must. Having to scroll to read the entire filename or to determine the extension is a real inconvenience to those you send to. The three main biggies you always need to consider are:

- Never put any spaces in the filename or the extension—this can make your file unreadable.

- Get in the habit of naming files in all small case. Caps or suffixes .GIF or .JPG may require that they be renamed in order to ensure they are useable/viewable.

- Only use alpha (abc) or numeric (123) characters. Punctuation, dashes, or other characters should not be used. You cannot use any of the following: " \ / : * < > ? ¦. A period can only be used before the suffix or extension, which must be three characters long.

SIDEBAR: For those with digital cameras, you will want to rename the file from the camera's default filename to be descriptive of each specific photo. All this requires is that when the file is opened on your system, you click on File then Save As, and rename that file to be descriptive of the subject of the photo. If you do not rename the camera-generated filename, you do run the risk of overwriting previous files that your camera designated with the same filename. Use descriptive filenames that note the content of the file. To just name them photo1, photo2 or photo3 requires that the recipient open them to determine what the photo subject is. In addition, in the future, you probably will not remember what the photos are of either. Descriptive filenames are a great help for those who receive attachments from various sources. If you receive files by e-mail, you will appreciate this as well.

DOCUMENTS AND SPREADSHEETS

●

People from different countries speak completely different languages. Similarly, different computer programs create their files in different formats unique to each program. A file created with WordPerfect might not be readable by Word for Windows. A file created with Lotus 123 might display wacky characters when viewed with Excel or may not even be able to be opened at all. Many of the newer programs have built-in translators for common file formats to help with this issue. Word for Windows will automatically try to translate a WordPerfect file, and vice versa. Often, these translators work pretty well. Occasionally, however, there are those wacky errors or gibberish characters that will display that make the file unreadable to the other party.

If you're exchanging files with others, you cannot be completely sure that whatever program they use will be able to read the files created by the program you use. Frustrating, right? Doesn't have to be! Avoid this unnecessary frustration by asking what program and version the other person uses in advance of sending it to them. If you both have the same program and version, you should not have any difficulties.

For word-processing documents in particular, if you don't use the same program or if you simply do not know what the other person is using, the best approach is to save your files to a format that both programs will most likely understand. Your word processor will usually have an option called "Save As . . . " which allows you to save a file in a different format other than the program's default. A program's default format is usually called its "native" format. In Word for Windows for example, that is a .doc extension. Often, different file formats are associated with different filename extensions. That is how your computer knows what software to use to open a file when you click on a filename.

Every word-processing program (and many other programs) can read files in "text" format (sometimes called "ASCII" format), which is noted by the file extension .txt. Text format, unfortunately, does not allow special layouts like tables, underlining, bolding, italics, etc. For this reason, there is a format that does try to preserve some formatting features. Word-processing programs can also read files in "rich-text format" (sometimes just called "rtf"), which is signified by the extension .rtf. RTF allows the saved file to hold more of the original document's formatting. What's the bottom line? For word-processing files that you're going to exchange with others, save them in both .txt and .rtf formats. If the recipient's program can read .rtf, then he or she will use that; if not, they will have the .txt file as an alternative. Just a good rule of thumb!

SIDEBAR: I can hear you Mac users—what about us? PCs are the majority online, and that is whom this chapter is targeted. PC users can get software that converts Mac files so they are readable on PCs. You Mac users know that Macs allow you to save files in "PC format," which still may not make the file viewable in any or all software on the other person's PC, but at the very least it is an effort worth making.

LEARN THE RIGHT WAY TO SEND FILES BY E-MAIL

•

Once you know how, it is easy to attach a file to an e-mail. Almost too easy! It shields you from the basic information you need to know before you send your attachment to the other person. Specifically information in regard to the file's size and format. When it comes to a file's size, you can view the file's size in Windows Explorer. Make sure the List option at the top menu bar is set to Details so that the file sizes are displayed. There you will see a "Size" column. When considering e-mailing any file over two hundred kilobytes, either ask permission first to send the large file as well as what time is best to do so to ensure the recipient is expecting the file and then zip it up or reduce its size using any one of the available file-compression utilities available for these purposes.

Never send anyone an e-mail with an attachment about any-thing (especially your product or service), if the recipient did not specifically e-mail you for that information and you are responding to his or her request. If you send overly large files, you can possibly fill the other person's e-mail box and cause all subsequent e-mail to bounce. Wouldn't that leave a poor impression? Many e-mail accounts are only five to ten megabytes in size and can be filled up very easily by those who either don't care to or don't know how to deter-mine file size and either minimize or compress the file to make it more manageable. Files over one megabyte should not be sent by e-mail and will have a hard time going through the pipeline if at all.

To include a large attachment someone didn't ask for is the epitome of lack of courtesy for those you are e-mailing, and your actions will most certainly leave a negative effect on the perception of your level of tech savvy. Common courtesies go a long way online when trying to foster relationships of any kind. Include an overly large attachment that is not com-pressed or in a format that requires one have the same soft-ware as you do (don't count on the fact they do) will cause those on the other side to wonder what else you do not con-sider important. Files should only be sent in a format that you know the other side has the appropriate software to view—because you asked first! Believe it or not, not everyone has MS Publisher, Excel, or PowerPoint.

SIDEBAR: When it comes to graphics, just assume the file is gargantuan. Whether it is business or personal you need to compress either the file's size with a program that com-presses files for these purposes or reduce the physical size of the graphic itself. Learn how to use your graphic software to resample/resize the image to no larger than six hundred pixels in width. That size is large enough for the majority of uses—especially if you are just sharing photos with friends or family. For use on your Web site, they need not be larger than this either or you could slow the download of your site. Photos that are thousands of pixels wide easily can get up into the two- to four-megabyte range—yikes!

LEARN HOW TO ORGANIZE YOUR FILES

•

I recently came across an article that mentioned a study which claimed computer users typically spend a great deal of their time searching for previously stored documents and data. Most computer users do not know where their files are! If they download files, they have no clue where they are downloaded to. This is not only unproductive but a very frustrating activity that ranks among the most time-consuming for those working with computers. No time like the present to learn! Here are some basic tips to help you get your files organized:

- Can't find a file? To find a file (data or document), go to Start, Find Files or Search. Then, type in the filename or any of terms you think the file is named with, and your computer will find all data with that information. Choose the one you want, and the appropriate program will open it.

- Save all your data in one folder, such as "My Documents" or one I use quite often is the folder I created named "Downloads," so that everything I download, I direct to that folder. For your Web site, create a folder called "Web site." For your photos—"My Photos." Use whatever works for you so that you will intuitively remember what you put where. You can create a folder on your C: drive by going into Windows Explorer, click on C (or an already established folder like "My Documents"). Once you have clicked on the location of where you would like to create a new folder, click on File, then New, then Folder, and a new folder will appear that you can name intuitively to suit your purposes. Want to rename a folder? Simply right click on its name and choose Rename.

- You can create folders within My Documents for each program, e.g., Docs (Word), PPT (Power Point), Excel, Photos, Attorney, Accountant, Home, Office, etc. This is a great idea to keep all your printed materials in one central location on your computer.

- When you want to save a new file, go to File, then Save As, and not only name the file properly so that you will recognize the file's contents at a later date, but save it in the appropriate location right off the bat!

- Name your files so they are short, descriptive, and intuitive.

Yes, you can ignore all this information, and your computer will allow you to have filenames that are up to 255 characters. And that is just dandy if the file is remaining on your computer for your eyes only. But when you want to send to others either for business or just to share information with friends or family via e-mail, renaming the files to shorter names and checking to ensure their size is manageable will make sure that those with whom you are communicating will want to continue to do so!

CYBERPARENTING 101

Many parental units are not "techies" and openly admit they are not. They seem to use that as an excuse to not be informed and "trust" their children to do what is right in an environment that is clearly risky. When it comes to underage children being online, there should be a set of household rules that are in place and followed, or the alternative is no online connections are allowed.

Parenting (n):

> The rearing of a child or children, especially the care, love, and guidance given by a parent. One who begets, gives birth to, or nurtures and raises a child.

Nothing there about "except when they are online." Here are my suggestions for those techno-challenged parental units who need to get involved and concerned about their children's online activities:

1. Keep your computer in an open place, such as the family room or rec room. No negotiation here! Online activities are only allowed in this public area and only when you are home. Allow a computer connected to the Internet behind a teenager's closed bedroom door or when you are not around to monitor their activities and you are asking for trouble!

2. Approve your children's e-mail addresses or handles.

You certainly do not want them using anything suggestive or what they perceive as "cool" that can lead to a negative or possibly dangerous perception. Examples of e-mail addresses or usernames that I have seen used by minors that I just know their parental units are unaware of include "big_daddy_pimp," "babythug," "toocute4u," "jokerXXX"—you get the idea. I do not think any responsible parent would want their child to be identified in this manner when online.

3. Keep your computer and online connection password protected. Use passwords that cannot be guessed by ingenious teenagers. This way, if you are preoccupied or not home, online access is not possible. Change your password on a regular basis when they are not around. Better safe than sorry!

4. Advise your children that they are not to give out their full name, address, city, state, and phone to anyone for any reason when online. Those whom they know in their off-line world get this info through traditional means. There is no reason whatsoever to give out this type of personally identifiable information online to anyone without your knowledge and supervision.

5. Learn as much as you can about the Internet, how it really works, including how to use your computer and browser so that you are aware of the potential problems your kids can run into. After they are online, use the drop-down bar in your browser's location bar to get a hint of what they have been up to. I have all kinds of mini-guides and easy-to-use tools to help you get up to speed with technology on my Web site: http://www.BuyTechieStuff.com. When placing your order, be sure to use discount code "bnmbook" to receive a 10 percent discount!

Be sure to install any one of the many filtering software packages that help prevent your children from being exposed to topics that would make even you blush. That said, software is only a tool—not a replacement for your personal involvement and genuine interest.

You hear stories in the news all the time about police stings, pedophiles making contact with children, or wacky teenagers running away to hook up with their newly discovered online love. If you remember, and are honest about it, as teenagers we didn't know squat in regard to communicating with strangers or what "love" is. Heck, I thought I was in love with Bobby Sherman!

For underage children, their life experience is simply not yet in place to make mature decisions. That's part of life, and your children need you to be their guide as they use technology. Watching over your children's online sessions is not an invasion of privacy—offspring do not have privacy until they are eighteen and move out! (Or is that around thirty nowadays?)

Online monitoring is a sign of a caring parent who is involved in the activities and information their children will be exposed to online. Yes, it may be frustrating for your children as they strive for more independence and as well for you as the parent as it will require all involved, learning some new things along the way. One simple rule to protect your children is this: Parental units need to be there to spend the time to monitor what their children are up to or the children are not allowed online access. A computer with an online connection is not a babysitter or, because we didn't have computers as children, an excuse to not be involved.

Learn, get involved, and be part of your children's online experiences. Look at it as another activity you can share together!

BUSINESS E-MAIL BASICS

This book and OnlineNetiquette.com have a cross mix of technology orientation and the basics of participating in technology with courtesy and knowledge. It is targeted at those new to the online arena, inexperienced with the nuances of e-mail, and those who sincerely care how they will be perceived and are willing to learn new things. For you, personally, when it comes to perception, the person on the other side of the screen does not know you and who really cares. With business, however, you need to care about the type of impression you make that can very well determine if someone will do business with you or not.

This chapter is solely targeted at businessmen, businesswomen, and e-mail. These are the issues business owners minimally need to be aware of in their online communications. And they shouldn't look at these guidelines as only for them but if they run or own a business; their employees need to master these issues as well, or it could cost them opportunity. Command of your e-mail skills goes a long way toward forging the most professional perception you can with any potential customer you may communicate with via e-mail.

Although these business e-mail basics are not the end-all, be-all, they can certainly ensure you avoid lost opportunity and negative perceptions due to improper e-mail habits.

1. *Subject* **Field:** Many folks determine even if they are going to open an e-mail by the **Subject** field. If this is your first contact with an associate based on their re-

quest through your site or otherwise, be sure to have a short and sweet subject that indicates clearly and specifically what the topic of the e-mail is. Never be misleading in this regard. Be sure to type the subject using proper upper- and lowercase, noting exactly what your e-mail is about. For example, if you sell widgets it could be: "Widget Information You Requested." The subject field is the window into your e-mail and can make or break you. Typos, all caps, or all-small case can give the impression you are a spammer—or worse yet, someone who isn't literate enough to want to do business with. Always put forth the effort to ensure that the **Subject** field is accurate and clear about the content of your e-mail. If the conversation is ongoing back and forth and the focus changes direction, make a point of changing the **Subject** field to reflect the conversation's new direction. Example: "**Subject:** Pricelist Enclosed. Was: Widget Information You Requested." Never use an old e-mail with a subject reflecting previous conversations and hit Reply and start typing about something unrelated. Make a point of adding all your important contacts to your address book, and create a new message when contacting them for a new discussion. Using old messages for new conversations gives the impression of lazy and not even knowing how to use your e-mail program.

2. **Level of Formality:** Never assume a position of informality in your business e-mail. Only time and relationship-building efforts can guide when you can begin to communicate in a more relaxed tone when it comes to your business relationships. In some cases, that time may never arise. Some customers will always prefer formalities while others will indicate a more relaxed tone is acceptable. Let each individual client guide you on what they prefer. Do not assume that e-mail is imper-

sonal or informal in your business communications. It is very personal—a window into the type of person you are, the type of person you would be like to do business with or not. For commercial/business reasons, one should communicate at all times as if the e-mail were on their company letterhead. This is your business's image you are branding! To prematurely communicate informally in a professional relationship, regardless of mode of communication used, can cause a negative perception with those whom you have not yet solidified your relationship with.

3. **Addressing:** How do you address your new contacts? I would suggest you assume the highest level of courtesy (Hello, Mr. Anderson; Dear Ms. Smith; Dr. Osborne; etc.) until your new contact states "call me John" or "you can call me Jane," keep it formal until it is clear the relationship dictates otherwise. You will be able to get clues of the level of formality they expect or prefer by how they communicate with you in their tone and how they sign off their e-mails. For example, I use *Judi* and *Judith* depending on the client and the relationship. Some clients actually prefer to call me Judith—fine. While others have picked up on my signature noting Judi and fall right into a more relaxed e-mail relationship. Most business people do not mind being called by their first name; however, in a global economy that can be perceived as taking premature liberties in the relationship and have a negative impact. So before presuming, as an example, it will always be courteous to ask "May I call you Judi? Or do you prefer Judith?" to determine what would be the best way to address your customer based on their preference. Also make the effort to be sure you are spelling their name correctly to show you pay attention to details. I get e-mail all the time addressed to "Judy" and that is not how I spell my name.

4. *To, From, Bcc, Cc* Fields Can Make or Break You:

- In the **To** field, be sure to have your contact's name formally typed. Example: John B. Doe—not *john b doe* or *JOHN B DOE.*

- In the **From** field, be sure to have your name formally displayed. Example: Jane A. Doe—not *jane a doe* or *JANE A DOE.* The latter two give the perception of lack of education or limited experience with technology.

- **BCC**. Use this field when e-mailing a group of contacts who do not personally know each other or is it not important to the message that all know who was sent a copy. By listing an arm's length list of e-mail addresses of contacts who do not know each other or have never met in the **CC** or **To** field is conducive to publishing their e-mail address to strangers. No matter how great the list of people may be to you, never make this decision for others! This is a privacy issue! With those you are forging partnerships with, listing their e-mail address in with a group of strangers will make one wonder what other privacy issues you do not respect or understand. Not good.

- **CC**. This field is used when there is a handful of associates involved in a discussion that requires they all be on the same page. If your name is in the **CC** field, this is an FYI, and a response from you is generally not expected. Those in the **CC** field are business people who know each other or have been introduced and you know they have no problem having their e-

mail address exposed to the parties involved.
If you are not sure if a business associate would
mind their address being made public, ask!

SIDEBAR: Keep in mind that when sending e-mail while on company time, the content and tone should reflect the level of professionalism your employer would expect. Forwarding of off-color jokes, personal e-mails, etc., while on company time—worse yet using a company e-mail address—can breach established company policies and at the very least reflect your lack of business savvy and respect for your employer. Keep personal e-mail and the forwarding of e-mail that is not work/job related for when you are not on the job. Never make the mistake of assuming what you may think is humorous will be accepted in kind by your fellow employees or your employer.

5. **Formatting:** Refrain from using it in your business communications. Unless you would type something in bold blue fancy-font letters on business letterhead, you don't do it when e-mailing for commercial gain. Not only is this viewed as amateurish, it also makes you look like the spammers or snake-oil e-mailers that all too often fill our inboxes. Keep in mind that your recipients may not have their e-mail program configured in such a way as to display your formatting the way you would like—if at all. Business communications rely on your ability to communicate with clarity using proper vocabulary, punctuation, and grammar—not formatting your name to be bright blue.

6. **Attachments:** All e-mail accounts have capacity limits. Do you think your relationship with a potential new customer is enhanced when you send them that five-megabyte PowerPoint presentation they didn't request

and you fill up their inbox shutting down their e-mail causing subsequent business correspondence to bounce as undeliverable? Nope. Add to that, if they don't have PowerPoint they wouldn't be able to open the file anyway! Do not assume your potential customers have the software you have to open any file you may arbitrarily send. First, let's get this one point straight. Just because you can physically instruct a computer to attach a file of that size doesn't mean you should. You could also instruct your computer to reformat/erase your hard drive but you don't do so, do you?

Attachments use the recipient's resources. Sending unnecessary, unexpected attachments reflects a lack of consideration for the person on the other side. Worse yet, sending of such attachments outside of business hours when the person on the other side is not there to keep their inbox clear shows a complete lack of courtesy. Sending attachments in this manner will show your lack of understanding from storage to download time to having to use system memory to open them. If your attachment holds a brief or simple announcement that can easily be cut-and-pasted within an e-mail, don't send it as an attachment and unnecessarily use the other side's possibly limited resources.

If you ever need to send a file over two hundred thousand bytes in size, you need to compress it or zip it up. There are several programs available for these purposes. Even then, business courtesy dictates you ask the recipient first if it is OK to send your attachments. The first thing you want to do is to confirm they have the same software/version you do. Next, ask the person you are sending to what the best time of day would be for you to send your attachment, and make a point of being prompt and sending it at that prearranged time. This little extra effort will make a big impression as you extend an uncommon courtesy to the recipient so that they can be available to download your large file and keep their e-mail flowing. Noting the file size in your request is a nice additional touch that will truly show your command of technology use. Never send large attachments without warning or on weekends when the recipient won't be there to clear out their e-mail box and keep their e-mail inbox free.

One cannot discuss attachments without bringing up viruses. Give a possible or current customer a destructive virus or get infected yourself with a virus that sends out e-mail from your computer to those addresses on your system and your chances of forming a positive relationship will be minimized.

7. **Down Edit Your Replies:** Don't just hit Reply and start typing. E-mail editing is a skill that takes time, diligence, and effort to master. This is a skill those you communicate with will appreciate, as it lends to reflecting clarity in your communications and a respect for their time. Removing parts of the previous e-mail that simply do not apply or add to your response including e-mail headers and signature files removes the clutter and keeps the conversation on track with fewer misunderstandings.

8. **Using Previous E-mail for New Correspondence:** If you want to give the perception of lazy, find a previous e-mail from the party you want to communicate with, hit Reply and start typing about something completely irrelevant to the old e-mail's subject. If you are not responding to that specific e-mail, you need to start a new e-mail. Take a moment to learn how to add your

contacts to your address book with one click so you can send them new e-mails, with relevant **Subject** fields to the issues contained with.

9. **Common Courtesy:** Hello, Good Day, Good Morning, Thank You, Sincerely, Best Regards. All these intros and sign offs that are a staple of professional business communications should also be used in your business e-mail communications. They lend a nice professional touch that many of your competitors feel are not necessary. Always have a salutation and sign off with every e-mail. Here again—think business letterhead!

10. **UCE or Spam:** Never ever send anything to anyone that they did not request you send about your business. This is called spamming and can get your company's e-mail and hosting account cancelled and blacklisted within the global network making e-mailing you or visiting your Web site very difficult or even impossible. No matter how great you think your product or service is, you must use legitimate practices to market yourself online. Sending UCE (Unsolicited Commercial E-mail) is definitely not one of them. This includes whether you are sending your "pitch" by e-mail or going to Web sites and using their resources and forms to send promotions they did not request.

11. **Signature Files:** Do not have an overly long signature file of more than four to six lines (including your sign-off and name) as this is viewed as a bit egocentric. Keep your signature file at around four to six lines, Web site link, company name, and slogan or phone number. Include a link to your site that the recipient can then visit to get all your contact information from A to Z including all your awards and associations—that is what your site is for.

Always include the "http://" when putting your Web site address within e-mails and your signature file. This will ensure it is recognized as a clickable URL regardless of the user's software, settings, or platform. If you include quotes in your signature file, be sure they are relative to your business or service. Famous quotations need to be used carefully, keeping in mind that quotes may not be appropriate for business communications, may reflect a personal opinion that your employer may not agree with, or that may inadvertently offend recipients.

The above tips will allow your business communications to rise above the majority who do not take the time to understand and master these issues. When forging new business relationships and solidifying established partnerships, the level of professionalism and courtesy you relay in your business e-mail communications will always gain clients over the competition that may be anemic, uninformed, or just plain lazy in this area. When it comes to business, regardless of mode of communication used, professionalism and courtesy never go out of style.

USING SIGNATURE FILES

Signature files have been around since, well, before most current Netizens were even aware that e-mail existed. Before the Web, most generally had basic contact info and included their favorite quote to indicate their feelings or perspective on certain issues. Now, most will use their signature file as a quick identifier of who they are and what they do and provide a link to their Web site. To this day, many online for personal use will still serve up witty, clever, and many times interesting quotes and commentary.

The most important reason to use a "sig" file is that signature files allow you to promote your site indirectly, by simply going about your daily online business communications. It also leaves a convenient link to your site in the inbox of recipients who keep your e-mail on file. Whether you are posting on message boards, e-mailing other site owners, or participating in mailing lists, your signature file gets your basic information and a link to your Web site in front of everyone you e-mail or those who may just read your post on a message board. Your "sig" file's contents can help you solidify yourself as an astute technology user and an ethical businessperson, as well as soft sell your business to your contacts. Signature files are the ultimate in online passive promotion when used properly and effectively.

LET'S FIRST COVER THE DON'TS

•

DON'T have your signature file start right after the last sentence line in your e-mail. This looks very unprofessional. Make a point of setting up an extra line break in your e-mail program, or just be sure to hit Enter one extra time when typing your e-mail is completed. Keep your sig file no more than four to six lines. No, there is no law that will send you to the pokey if you break this guideline; however, this is a rule that most follow and is a recommended guideline so you don't appear too overbearing.

DON'T have everything about you, including the kitchen sink, in your sig file. If you have a Web site, include a pointer to your URL to ensure the recipient can find out whatever they like about you—that is really what your sig file is for. To have your pager, cell, home, business, work, accreditations, and slogan about how great you are will lead to the perception that you are tad bit self-enclosed.

DON'T throw in any sales-pitchy-type hype. Credibility online is very difficult to attain and maintain without undermining your efforts. Refraining from overzealous sales hype that ends in exclamation marks tends to lead to you being perceived as a seasoned professional. A short and sweet comment about your product or service is sufficient. Let your Web site do the selling for you!

DON'T include formatting in your sig file (or your business e-mails), ASCII formatting, colors, or attaching any animated graphics. I've lost count of every formatted sig or e-mail that then messed with my reply by formatting it as well or worse yet by looking like doo-doo because I read all my mail in plain text. If you wouldn't turn your name or title bright blue on your company letterhead—don't do it in your e-mail. When aligning your sig's text, do so with spaces rather than tabbing. Tabs and text are displayed differently on different machines, which can make your layout look yucky. You want to keep your sig file to seventy characters or less, as that is the set screen width default for most e-mail programs.

DON'T close with your signature file reflecting anything but proper punctuation. Capitalize your name formally: John A. Doe, John Doe, or John. Not typing your name formally with appropriate capitalization reflects a lack of education and business savvy.

DON'T start using your sig file until you have verified, reviewed, and double-checked that all the information is correct. I see signature files with errors every day! Sigs with errors can contribute to the perception that you lack attention to detail.

NOW TO THE DO'S

●

DO make sure that your signature file contains the basic info a recipient needs to contact you. No need to include your e-mail address—that is automatically noted at the top of every e-mail you send. The only instance where you would want to include your primary e-mail address in your signature file is if you are using a different or secondary e-mail address to send the e-mail in question.

DO setup your e-mail program to automatically append your signature file and make sure to include your sign-off so that you do not have to type your name with every e-mail. So for example, you can have:

Thank you,
John A. Doe
Widgets Sprockets
http://WebSiteAddressHere.com
Slogan or Additional Information Here

DO make sure that you add the "http://" before your site's URL when you include your Web site address. In some e-mail programs, without the http://, the program may not recognize the address as a link, and it will not be clickable within your e-mail. One of the neat things about sig files is that they allow you to have every e-mail you send be only one click away from your Web site. Don't miss this opportunity by forgetting the "http://."

DO have several signatures that you can switch, dependent on tone or issue at hand. Sig files are an excellent way of setting a tone and direction of the ongoing communications priority or level of formality. *Sincerely, Best Regards,* and *Respectfully* can be used differently depending on whom you are communicating with and the tone you would like to set. You can also set up signatures that have your formal name and a less informal version to set a comfort zone with the other party such as Elizabeth versus Lizzy. Keep in mind to not be overly informal too soon with new contacts. Formalities are in place for a reason—especially in business communications.

DO have signature files that relay a different message based on where and to whom you are e-mailing. If you are marketing on message boards or newsgroups, use a signature file that reflects your new product or the current promotion that is directed to that specific audience. Different terms and words have different affectivity depending on the market that views it. Be sure to include a call to action, such as "Download now . . . ." "Contact Us today about . . . ," "Get your trial account today . . . ," you get the idea—sans hype. Refrain from using multiple exclamation marks or question marks. The beauty of your sig file is that you do not have to say anything about your own site in the body of a posting . . . unless it would be relevant or appropriate to the discussion and it is the proper forum. Signature files are a great way to subtlety market to those you do not know. Keep in mind, however, the last thing you want to do is post gratuitously or send an e-mail with a one-word answer just for the sake of getting your signature file in front of readers. That is one of the oldest tricks in the book and the other more experienced members will know what you are up to and may complain directly to you and/or the moderator. Credibility lost.

DO keep in mind that the perception your signature file gives will lead to the perception of who you are, what you believe in, if you follow the rules, if you know how to use technology or not. Quotes are fine and sometimes apropos depending on the conversation's tone and topic; however, remember who will be reading the e-mail and the perception your opinion via the quote you include will leave. Humorous quotes are best left to personal e-mail.

So there you have it. The basics you need to know to use signature files properly and effectively. Use these tips to build your own personal library of signature files. I have over seventy-five myself! Always update and work on your signature files—there is always something new to say about yourself or your business!

HOW TO DEAL WITH RUDE E-MAILERS

Not sure if it is the unusually strong solar flares, full moon, or the fact Mars was closer to Earth that it has been or will be for thousands of years. Rude and crass e-mail seems to be at an all time high. E-mails blurting out demands or questions without the courtesy of a decent subject field or a thank you to follow. Questions or requests that are demanding a reply with typos galore, no courtesy of a hello, or a closing that indicates the sender's name unfortunately are all too common.

Could it be because manners seem to be at an all-time low off-line? Combine this with so many onliners who apparently do not realize the power of the written word or have the skills to communicate clearly to reflect their tone and intent and you have a volatile combination.

There are two assumptions here. The first being that anything goes online—there are no rules, you can do what you want—period, and don't try to tell them differently! As any Web site owner will eventually experience, I have been spammed numerous times through OnlineNetiquette.com's contact form by site visitors typing in caps and using profanities questioning my intent, my content, and my opinions. I didn't make these folks come to my site and read it—all they had to do was hit the Back button and go find a site that agrees with them.

One visitor actually asked, "Who did I think I was even imply-
ing that folks have to be courteous if they didn't want to?" I
was then told "The Internet is a 'free-for-all' and there are no
rules!!" Typical of those who e-mail in that manner, their pro-
test e-mails used bogus e-mail addresses so I could not respond or report them for e-mailing threats and profanities.
Those who react in this manner to what they don't want to
hear or do seemingly have personality disorders. In my not-
so-humble opinion (IMNSHO), if you do not have the courage
to identify yourself with a valid e-mail address, your opinion is
moot.

Secondly, and a big contributor, is the belief that there is no
good reason (even if there actually is one) for anyone to not
say what they want, when they want, claiming "freedom of
speech." Let's get this "freedom of speech" issue clarified
once and for all! The "freedom of speech" guaranteed by the
U.S. Constitution only protects you from *governmental inter-
vention* in your right to express yourself. It does not give one
free reign to use computer resources against the wishes of
their owner or to say what they want in scurrilous terms when
hiding behind a computer screen.

Consideration for other's feelings and opinions don't seem to
matter when you can tap out some uninformed crudeness
and hit Send. Folks are quite bold in the anonymity that being
behind their computer screen offers them. Some fly off the
handle without reading an entire site, article, thread, or e-
mail, many times picking out parts to create a manifesto of
uninformed opposition without actually looking at the big picture of the topic at hand. Those who are not conversant combined with lack of attention to detail do not hesitate to spew
their self-important opinions that many times are not based
in fact or reality. Misunderstandings occur, business is lost,
and feelings get hurt. All of which are due to onliners not

taking the time to communicate carefully with the written word by integrating courtesy and clarity.

What do you do when you are the recipient of an e-mail with an accusatory or rude tone? Well, I used to be a firm believer that you should respond to every e-mail someone takes the time to send you—that is, everything but spam. However, as of late, I have even found myself at a loss for words when reading some of the e-mail that has come my way. Folks who don't know me or even those who do and should know better, coming off as terse, making accusations or using verbiage that makes my cheeks flush!

Unfortunately, I think all of us will have to deal with these "personalities" at one time or another and probably more so that any of us prefer. Here are some thoughts to help you determine if and how to deal with rude or nasty e-mail.

- If you receive an e-mail with foul language or threats, know that this is against the TOS (Terms of Service) of all ISPs. Immediately send the full e-mail to abuse@ at their ISP. Keep the e-mail on file in case you need to refer to it or provide additional copies down the road. If they use their own dot-com as their e-mail address, check at your favorite registrar for the DNS servers where their dot-com is hosted and report them to their hosting company.

- When you receive an e-mail that is blatantly rude or obnoxious and is not based in fact, think about if there is any constructive reason to have to respond. If the tone is so rude that you feel your blood pressure rise, wait until the next morning at the very least to even think about if you need to respond at all. Your ego is not large enough (I hope) to have the need to defend yourself when faced with incorrect accusations or personal digs, especially from onliners who don't know you. Don't lower yourself to their level by responding to this type of e-mail in kind. Hold yourself to a higher ground and do not respond at all, regardless of the tone or accusations used.

- If someone e-mails you because they are misinformed, did not take the time to read the information on your site or a post somewhere online, or possibly could have made an honest mistake, reply to them with kindness and give them the benefit of the doubt. Most truly do not know how they are perceived by virtue of their lack of e-mail skills, and believe it or not, nor do they expect you to take them at their word. All too often, when it comes to e-mail misunderstandings, I hear, "I didn't mean it that way . . . Well, I have a saying around here, if you type it, you better mean it!

- Onliners who e-mail in this manner simply do not realize the power of their words and the tone they are setting. Point out in a courteous manner the information to correct the issue or point them to the area on your site or elsewhere that has the information they seek without personalizing the issue. Thank them for contacting you, sign off in a professional manner, and hold your head high knowing you just provided a level of courtesy that is quite rare online. You may even be surprised when that very same Netizen sends you a thank-you e-mail! That being said, with some onliners there is nothing you can do to sway them. You can be correct, courteous, and clear and it won't matter—they simply will not admit to being misinformed or plain old wrong. Don't take it personally—feel sorry for anyone with a mind that closed and move on.

- Because you have a Web site, are visible in online forums, or are available via e-mail in no way means that you have the responsibility to respond to those who do not communicate with you in a respectful, courteous manner. And most likely those who do not communicate with courtesy and knowledge are folks most of us would not care to form a relationship with or do business with anyway. So don't let worrying about losing that online "friend" or business "lead" have you lower your standards in regard to how you want to be treated.

I receive more e-mails than most onliners in a given day. Most are positive and many are simply wonderful written by great people across the globe that have been to one of my sites and are asking my assistance or advice. Some even taking the time to send a simple compliment—how nice is that!? However, for those increasing number of folks who think they can just e-mail and make accusations, demands, or requests without a hint of courtesy or consideration, well, they won't be hearing from me—DELETE!

TEN E-MAIL
ORGANIZATION TIPS

Who hasn't experienced the challenges of organizing their inbox!? I receive a ton of e-mail throughout each day due to the variety of activities and contacts I have online. Some I am truly interested in their content; many I am not.

A big part of keeping your inbox and your e-mail organized is discipline. Yep, good ole-fashioned discipline! You need to make a consistent practice of checking your e-mail and accomplishing several tasks on a daily basis just to keep ahead of the increased traffic of bits and bytes finding their way to your inbox. What are we to do? Let's get organized!

1. Put your Delete button to work! If you don't recognize the sender, look at the **Subject** field. Are there funny characters, alpha-numeric gibberish, misspelled words, or it just doesn't make sense? Delete! Don't fall for the latest tricks of **Subject** fields that say any number of enticing comments only a friend would say: "Did you get my last e-mail . . . ," "They said it's free!" "Hey, how is it going?" "You blocked my IM," "Please don't be angry about yesterday," or the one almost everyone wants to open "About Your Tax Refund." None of these are from friends or folks you know or even companies you are doing business with. They are from spammers—the worst kind too—the ones who underestimate your intelligence by thinking these e-mails will be something you would take seriously. Don't know

the sender, **Subject** field looks wacky? Send them on their way to the trash!

2. Once you go through all your new e-mail and follow step no. 1 above, you are now ready to determine what to do with the e-mails that are left. Do you have several e-mails from the same party? Do you have e-mail from onliners who e-mail you quite regularly? Do you have some e-mail that is personal business and others that are more serious and therefore you probably need to keep a copy on hand? This is where filters come in. Filters are your friends! Filters, or Rules as they are called in Outlook, are what allow you to organize your e-mail on the download. Yes, as you download your e-mail, it can go into e-mail folders setup for specific topics or contacts!

You can have a "Mom" filter that sends all e-mail from dear old Mom right into your "Mom" folder. Set up filters to have e-mail from some of your hobby sites, go directly into their own folder. Your best friend can have his or her own folder. Another example is to have information from your financial institutions automatically end up in a folder specifically divided into further folders—Annuity, CDs, Stock, Bonds. The sky is the limit! A side benefit of filters is that if you organize your e-mail to go into their own folders on the download, your inbox has less e-mail that you requested or were expecting leaving only the questionable e-mail for you to review.

Filters only need be setup once, and they are in place until you delete them. Get your filters tightly setup and you can literally find only e-mail from spammers are left in your inbox. You can learn about filters/rules in the Help section of your e-mail program. One thing is clear about being online and e-mailing—it behooves you to become familiar and proficient with your tools. E-mail software being probably the most important. You can also go to the Web site for your e-mail software to get further guidance on filters or rules. This is reading and skill-building well worth the time when you realize how easily you can control your e-mail's organization moving forward.

3. Another use for your filters? As if filters are not already sounding like the best thing since sliced bread, you can use them to send certain e-mail right to the trash bypassing your inbox altogether! You know, the e-mails for enhancement products and adult sites—right to trash. Filters and rules can be used not only to send an e-mail to a certain folder by virtue of an e-mail address or company or person's name, they can be configured to find certain adult or offensive terms when listed in the **Subject** or body of an e-mail message and send them right to trash on the download—just got to love that—right to trash!

4. Back to your inbox. . . . We now have filters in place that organize your e-mail on the download so all the e-mails you requested and or are expecting are in their appropriate folders for you to read at your convenience. Now your inbox should only have the orphan e-mail with nowhere to go. After following the suggestions above, begin to review your e-mail. If you run into an e-mail that is from a new mailing list you've subscribed to and plan on getting regular e-mail from, stop right there and make a folder and filter to accommodate these future e-mail. Set up a filter to look for something specific to that e-mail (usually their e-mail address works best) and moving forward, on the down-

load, those e-mails will go right into their own folder. Do this for any e-mail topic or contact you plan to receive e-mail from on a regular basis.

5. Read and delete. Read your e-mail as time permits, and delete any e-mail that does not have content worth keeping for future reference. Loads of e-mail files use up your system's resources. Not keeping copies of e-mail you really will never need in the future helps remove the clutter and drain on system resources.

6. When reading your e-mail, you can prioritize when you want to address them. Many e-mail programs allow you to label e-mail by color when viewing a particular folder. For example you could have labels that at a glance tell you how you have prioritized your tasks. Say, red for *urgent*, blue for *later*, yellow for *maybe*. By opening that specific folder you know, at a glance, which e-mail you have set to address right away and which you can get to as time permits.

7. Empty your trash daily; but before emptying your trash, you want to be sure to take a quick look—see just in case any of your filters inadvertently picked up on something included in an e-mail that you possibly didn't want to trash. This happens all the time. A quick once-over before deleting your trash will ensure legitimate e-mail you do want to see didn't get lost in the shuffle.

8. Create a folder called Follow-Up, Interesting, or To Do. This is where you will file some of the e-mail from your inbox that peaked your interest that you would like to review in more detail but just don't have the time. Then, when time permits, you can go to that folder and check into the e-mails worth keeping. Once you review them,

though, either send them to another folder for keeps or send them to trash.

9. To avoid e-mail backup, be sure your inbox is cleared each day. Move e-mail to trash, a specific folder, or your "To Do" folder, and then empty the trash. If e-mail is older than thirty days in your "To Do" folder, send them off to trash as most likely the information or offer is no longer current. By doing so each day, you keep your inbox clear and your e-mail much more organized.

10. What about all these folders? Have as many folders as you need to be organized, and call them whatever will intuitively work for you with a glance. This system is different and unique to each and every user—make sure you use terms and a system that works for you.

The above ten tips when practiced daily will make the world of difference in keeping your inbox organized and clutter free. Just a bit of discipline is all it takes to be on the road to less time spent dealing with e-mail which frees you up to do other important things . . . like responding to e-mail.

THINK BEFORE YOU FORWARD . . .

A simple checklist of things to consider before forwarding e-mail:

✓ If the e-mail was forwarded to you, be sure to remove any e-mail addresses of those you do not know before you forward again and possibly expose them to folks they don't know. This is a serious privacy issue that you want to avoid problems with.

✓ If you are forwarding to a group of folks who do not know each other, put all their e-mail addresses in the **BCC** field.

✓ If the e-mail has been forwarded and forwarded and forwarded and scrolling forever, at the very least down edit all the >>>>>> and any other header or previous e-mail information that is not the actual guts of the e-mail you want to forward. Only forward the actual content—not all the previous e-mail notes and forward from the multitude of others who have no e-mail skills.

✓ If you will be forwarding an attachment, check the file size first before you just plop it into someone's inbox. Just because some knucklehead forwarded an extremely large file to you doesn't mean you do the same. If you don't know how to tell the size of the file, learn how. If the file is over two hundred kilobytes, compress it or e-mail the person you would like to forward it to first asking when would be the best time to send it to them.

✓ Never just forward without a comment. If you cannot take the time to type a "Hey, Jack, you'll love this! Love, Cindi" or "Howdy, Oscar—thought of you when I saw this—enjoy!" or "TTYS, John," then don't bother. If you can't take the time to jot down a quick howdy to the person you are forwarding to, then don't forward at all. For business e-mail, this is even more important! You'll come off bossy or inconsiderate forwarding e-mail that is business oriented without giving the recipient your thoughts or request.

✓ Jokes can be funny, but make sure what your tickles your sense of humor will have the same effect on those you forward to. Not everything that cracks you up will do the same when received on the other side. And a word of caution: be very careful about forwarding anything "colorful" through your work/employer's computer on their time.

✓ If you are forwarding something that you would like the other side to comment on, let them know that—specifically and then TIA!—thank them in advance.

Forwarding of e-mail is easy, just push a button and a click in your address book and very little thought goes into sending that e-mail on its way—and all too often it appears as though no thought was given before doing so. Let those you communicate with know why you are sending them the e-mail which will reflect courtesy for their time cultivating strong online relationships that you will cherish for years. Plus, you'll be setting a good example!

HOW TO IDENTIFY AND HANDLE SPAM/UCE

Spam or UCE (Unsolicited Commercial E-mail) is the online equivalent to off-line junk mail. The difference being off-line, one must identify their market and purchase a targeted mailing list to be effective. They also must incur the cost of the printed materials of which the quality will determine how they are perceived and the postage to snail mail them. Or they incur phone charges if calling folks during their dinner or busy day to sell them things they may not want or have any interest in.

Unlike the off-line world, online bulk e-mailers have no cost other than their time and an Internet connection to jam their poorly created scams and "opportunities" into the mailboxes of hundreds of thousands of Netizens per hour. Spamming is simply not the same as cold calling via telephone off-line (although many of us despise that practice just as much). It is, at best, annoying and, at worst, illegal in some states. No matter how legitimate you may feel your offer is, it's not legitimate if done over illegitimate channels. No matter how sincere your intentions may be, one can be sincerely naive participating in technology when they have not taken the time to understand it completely.

So that being said, regardless of your personal opinions, spam is not an accepted marketing practice online—period. Unfortunately, you will be receiving many e-mails to the contrary. By spamming, you risk getting your account canceled from your ISP, server company, and other technology partners or worse yet becoming blacklisted which will prevent network traffic from reaching your Web site.

Those who have had it with the intrusiveness of spam and have above-average technology expertise may take it upon themselves to "return fire," sending retaliatory spam, tracing the employment and personal information of the spammer, and generally doing some very nasty stuff. The spammer's personal information may even be posted online. By offending professionals and experts in the field (which you most likely will inevitably do), you are opening yourself up to the furor of those whose resources you waste. Spamming is most certainly not the way to build credibility for your venture.

Follow these tips to help you identify and deal with the spam you too will be receiving. From get-rich schemes or weight-loss miracles, getting a diploma online and even those pointing you to seemingly legitimate sites, just hit Delete!

- Successful, credible, and legitimate Web marketing or technology professionals will never spam you. Those who spam you about search engines, cheap Web design, etc. are not those you can count on to help you build a credible business because they build their business taking advantage of what others do not know. Those truly good at what they do are too busy assisting their growing client bases and have no need to blindly e-mail those they do not know or have not qualified. Whether it be the "guaranteed top ten" listings with Search Engines or the e-mails that cleverly have a subject that insinuates the sender knows you—they are all spam! Just hit Delete!

- As noted above, you need to understand that there are a plethora of individuals whose only job is to use your lack of knowledge to give a deceiving perception of quality and value—all to line their pockets. Then onto the online snake-oil salesmen; "Get Rich Quick," "Make Millions from Your Home," "Lose One Hundred Pounds in a Week Sitting on Your Couch," "University Diplomas" . . . Unless you personally know who sent you the e-mail, don't believe it! You know the saying, "If it sounds too good to be true"? That statement applies ten times online! Just hit Delete!

- If the e-mail is not addressed specifically to you (you@youre-mail.com) you have been spammed. Dead giveaways are the **To** field is empty or filled with anonymous e-mail accounts such as friend@ public.com or *trythis@nowhere.com.* Accounts with juno.com, yahoo.com, msn.com, or hotmail.com are free, throw-away accounts commonly used by spammers. The majority of e-mails originating from foreign countries are also typically spam. These individuals will spam, suck in what responders they can, cancel the account, and are never to be seen again. The **From** field will have an erroneous e-mail address too, either matching the **To** field address or showing another fake e-mail address. This is so you cannot track them down to complain about the spam or their products at a later date. Credible companies do not hide their identity. When reviewing the e-mail in your inbox, if **To** and **From** do not appear to be legitimate, it is a safe bet to just hit Delete!

- When you receive spam that includes an apology stating something to the effect that if you want to be removed from the mailing list you need to hit Reply or send an e-mail with cancel or unsubscribe to a certain address, don't follow these instructions! If you do, you will risk confirming that there is a live body at the end of your e-mail address, only to receive more spam and to have your e-mail address sold even further. (Now of course this does not apply to those legitimate businesses to which you did sign up to get periodic updates. In those cases, yes, follow these instructions. This is all about using common sense and paying attention to details!)

Do not believe for a moment if the e-mail quotes some statute or law that claims they are not spamming and that it is OK for them to send you junk mail you did not ask for. No such law—remember, if it walks like a duck . . . These guys have software that sends out hundreds of thousands of e-mails per hour. They don't know who you are or even if your e-mail address is "fresh"—meaning active. Just hit Delete!

- If your own Web site uses autoresponders, you will get undeliverable-message e-mails when the autoresponder cannot deliver to the fake or forged return e-mail address used in the original spam sent through your site. Autoresponders have no way of knowing whether a request into your site is from a "real" or valid e-mail address—they just "automatically respond."

Every single e-mail that is returned to you as undeliverable will state very clearly in the top portion of the e-mail why it was returned. In the case of spam, "no such account/user," "unknown user," or "account is over quota or has been closed" are the common reasons noted. If you get autos returned because they could not be delivered, look within the returned message for the reason why.

There is so much going on with spamming and viruses; expect to get returned/undeliverable e-mails that you did not initiate. If you receive e-mail returns and they are returned from what are clearly fake addresses, don't bother your ISP or Web host with questions of "What is going on?" or claims that something is "wrong" with your Web site or server as though they have control over these returns—they don't. You were spammed by someone who used a bogus e-mail address, or a virus is at play from someone who had your e-mail address on their system. Nothing can be done about either. Just hit Delete!

- If you receive blank e-mails, one of several things can be happening:

    o Your e-mail is being tested to see if it bounces back as undeliverable so your address can be sold again—nothing you can do about that.

    o The spammer doesn't know how to code properly, causing the content of the e-mail to not be viewable. Legitimate professionals don't do this as they make sure their e-mail is readable by as many users as possible—that is just good business.

    o Someone who has your e-mail address in their address book has a virus.

Regardless of which of the three it may be, just hit **Delete**! Really, you are not missing anything!

- Don't believe the majority of spam that you read unless it comes from a qualified source that you specifically contacted for information. Just because an e-mail lands in your inbox does not give it one iota of credibility or legitimacy. If the above information applies and there is not a URL to a high-quality Web site for you to review, more of a reason to just hit **Delete**!

- There are all kinds of online resources on the legality and handling of spam. Most likely, your ISP has policies and a help area you should make yourself familiar with. There are a couple things you can do to keep your spam levels manageable (if there is such a thing):

  o Be very selective where you give out your e-mail address online. Always read a Web site's privacy policy to see if they will sell or provide your information to their "partners." If they do not give you the option to "opt-out" of them giving/selling/providing your information to others who have nothing to do with you doing business with them, then don't do business with them!

  o Use a Yahoo.com, MSN.com, or Juno.com e-mail address if you participate on mailing lists or discussion groups. Discussion groups are farmed by spammer software to get active e-mail addresses. Using a Yahoo.com, MSN.com, or Juno.com e-mail address gives you more flexibility down the road in getting a new e-mail address and stopping the spam rather than having your business's dot-com out there, which you most likely will never change.

  o Ask your Web developer about ways to shield or hide the e-mail addresses on your Web site to prevent them from being "farmed" by spammer, e-mail-gathering software. Another option is using a form script where the e-mail address cannot be farmed, rather than having e-mail links. This can make a big difference!!

  o Most Web site hosting servers have a "default" e-mail catchall that can be set to send e-mail the server doesn't know what to do with to a designated e-mail address for you to check. Spammers will use variations of your dot-com e-mail address to get as many copies to any particular dot-com as possible. Have your server setup to handle only established accounts that are set up on the server and disable the "default forward" if at all possible. This way if the account is not a setup account anything else @yourdomain.com that is not setup by you bounces back to the spammer as undeliverable.

o   Learn how to use your e-mail program's filters. Filters, based on the **To**, **From**, **Subject** or text within an e-mail, will send e-mail that meets the criteria you indicate directly to trash. This is also a great organizational tool for those who get a bunch of e-mail. For spam you can have, as an example, any e-mail with the word "sex" goes directly to trash on the download—you never even have to see it!

o   One thing to keep in mind is that before you bother your ISP, technology consultant, or the sender of the e-mail itself, you be sure that you have not in fact requested the information sent before you report or cause problems for legitimate enterprises simply responding to your request.

Spam is not going to go away. But empowered with information and a dash of diligence, you can minimize and ensure that the e-mail you receive is only that which you want to take the time to review because you requested it and expected its arrival.

TIPS TO STOP SPAM!

I get asked almost daily about how to minimize getting so much spam and if having your e-mail addresses/links on your site(s) (I've had requests from both business and personal sites.) can contribute to the amount of spam you can get. Yes and yes!

Offensive junk mail, in particular that of an adult nature, has become increasingly an issue to all of us onliners and site owners alike. Unfortunately, we are forced to deal with spam—whether we like it or not. And for the record, we don't like it! Until which time a law is passed or overseas ISPs become less greedy, there are steps you can take to minimize your exposure to this type of e-mail.

- Get to know how to use your e-mail program's filter features—filters are your friend! Set up e-mail filters for the terms that you find offensive, directing the e-mails in question to be delivered right to your trash on the download. Use variations of these terms even using small and large case combinations you simply do not want to see. Every e-mail program has the ability to set filters based on variables (**To**, **From**, **Subject**, text within the body) found within an e-mail. Learn how to use your program's filtering options so you are not exposed to these e-mails again. By filtering based on offensive terms, this spam goes right to trash!

- I do not recommend you have your e-mail address on the bottom of every page of your Web site as was common for years—this goes for personal and/or business pages. Spammers have sophisticated software that farms any e-mail address it can find on a Web site by looking for the code that produces the e-mail link. You can use ASCII coding to deter these efforts—although it may only be a temporary stop-gap. All you need to do is replace all the characters within your e-mail address with the alternative ASCII character. Here is a great resource for ASCII codes:

http://www.ascii.cl/htmlcodes.htm

o   Spam e-mail-address-farming software is running 24/7, scanning every online computer file that it runs across collecting e-mail addresses for the sole purpose of selling mailing lists. Then, adult sites, amongst many others, buy those lists. Nothing illegal going on here—maybe unethical as the adult site owners are not ensuring their e-mail is received by those who have a true interest in what they have to offer, but nothing we can do to stop this part of the process.

o   Another option is to remove the active e-mail addresses from every page of your personal and/ or business Web site and point visitors to your site's contact form. By doing so, you will avoid being "farmed" as often. There are all kinds of sites that offer free forms scripts that are easy to use for a novice and most hosting companies offer these kind of scripts with support too.

o   Now, don't panic! Some are concerned that site visitors will not contact them if they remove those e-mail links and make visitors use a form. This is simply not based on fact or pattern, or my experience in the ten years running my online consulting business. For a personal site, I do not believe you have to worry—your friends or visitors will fill out a short form. When it comes to a business site, how to qualify potential customers or leads based on a site contact is simply good business. The type of "customer" that would not contact you because they have to give you some basic information through a form versus blurting out their questions in an e-mail that an e-mail link produces tend to be not those you can turn into a profitable customer anyway. Qualifying potential customers is core to all successful businesses.

o   If you have a form that is user friendly and makes sense to the requests that would be initiated by your site, site visitors will complete the form. And you get the valuable information you need to provide a prompt and efficient reply. Just don't go overboard asking for everything including their shoe size when all they want to do is ask you about something on your site.

- Unless you know for a fact you have subscribed to receive e-mail or offers from a specific company, it is best to not respond to their unsubscribe instructions by hitting Reply. I agree, you should not have to unsub from something you didn't ask to get in the first place— but here again we have no choice. For those bottom-of-the-barrel spammers who instruct you to hit Reply and type "unsubscribe," you most likely will only confirm your address to be "fresh." These folks send out to tens of thousands if not hundreds of thousands of e-mails at a time. By e-mailing them back, they know your address is a live one to be kept on the lists to be sold again, and again, and again.

o I am not saying all companies work like this. You can tell the cheeseball gimmick e-mails from those legitimate (and I use that term loosely for those who spam) businesses trying to get exposure in your inbox. As with most issues online, use your common sense!

o *Please note:* There are unsub procedures from mailing lists or companies that you *did* sign up for that are valid and effective procedures. This recommendation only applies to those that are sending to you without your previous permission. Make a point when voluntarily signing up for notices or announcements that you keep their confirmation e-mail in a separate folder for future reference. These confirmation e-mails will generally confirm your subscriptions and included opt-out information and instructions.

- Use a Yahoo!, Hotmail, or other free Web-based e-mail account to subscribe to mailing lists and public discussion groups. These areas are where a great deal of e-mail-address farming is accomplished. If you find you are getting too much spam to that address, shut it down and create a new address. But remember, when doing so, that you will have to resubscribe to all the announcements and mailing lists that you do want to continue to receive. They will not know your new address unless you resub and/or advise them.

Spamming is not going to cease for the foreseeable future. Until the Internet community at large makes it clear to business owners, ISPs, and hosting companies, many of who are located overseas beyond the reach of laws and legislation and our opinions on the issue, that this practice is not to be tolerated, not much will be changing. I receive tons of spam each day from enlarging certain portions of my anatomy (That I don't even possess!), to work-at-home schemes, how to lose weight, and every MLM or scam in between. This makes me ask two things:

- Are there really that many businesses who think I will believe this junk?

- Are there really that many onliners that believe this junk?

Unfortunately, the answer to both of those questions seems to be "yes." So when you get approached, remember that saying "if it sounds too good to be true, it is!" Do not believe everything you read. When you receive an e-mail that interests you, do your due diligence—check them out, ask for references. Look at the quality of their Web site from visuals to content which many times are very telling in regard to the enterprise's investment in its own online presence and their business savvy and professionalism. Search out a guarantee and privacy statement while also looking for what reliable associations they belong to so as to boost their credibility. If you have questions or want to confirm their return- or online-shopping-guarantee policy, e-mail them then judge them on how long it takes for them to respond and the quality of their response. Do they practice proper Netiquette? Check with the Better Business Bureau at bbb.org before you send any company money to see what their record is. If they don't have a Web site, that's a big clue!

If you are sick of spam, do what I do—report them and get their accounts cancelled. I use a great service called SpamCop (*http://www.spamcop.net*) that is free and also offers a more feature-rich subscription for a small fee. I pay for a subscription to the site because I feel if I use a service enough, it is important to help support their efforts. The paid service gives you a SpamCop e-mail address so you can filter all your e-mails through the SpamCop site to alleviate much of the spam from ever making it to your inbox.

With this service, accounts can be cancelled due to complaints generated by the Spam Cop site. I know alone I am not making a dent in the spam out there—but there is nothing like getting that e-mail with the words:

> *"Thank you for making us aware of these activities.*
> *This user's account has been cancelled."*

Cheap thrills—get them where you can!

HOW NOT TO LOOK SPAMMY

Who hasn't complained about the amount and type of junk e-mail they get on a daily basis? Then, turn the tables and realize that you need to make sure that the e-mails you send are not misidentified as possible spam. With just a little extra effort and by following these simple tips you can make sure your e-mail makes it to your intended party without them (or their spam filters) sending you to trash.

1. Always include an appropriate, short, and accurate **Subject**. Many times spam does not have a **Subject,** or it is ridiculously mangled. Many e-mail programs auto delete e-mail with mangled or empty subject fields to junk/trash. I receive so many subjectless e-mails; I no longer can take the time to look through all of them to determine "if" one is a legitimate e-mail.

2. Type your subject with appropriate capitalization. All-small case or all-large case gives the impression of being spam.

3. Make sure your name is formally displayed in the **From** field. Example: Jane A. Doe is correct—not: jane a doe, jane, or JANE. Lowercased or lack of punctuation here indicates lack of online savvy and that your e-mail could be spam.

4. Refrain from using common terms abused by spammers in your subject and/or first paragraph of your e-mail.

Many spam filters track these terms and may inadvertently send your e-mail right to trash. Here are several things to avoid using in your e-mail so you do not unintentionally trip spam filters:

- Avoid these terms as the first word in your **Subject**: Help, Get, Free, Try, Create, You, New, Hi.

- Avoid these phrases in your **Subject**: check this out, see this, visit our Web site.

- Avoid using *free*, *Free*, *FREE*, *guarantee*, *credit card*, *sex*, etc. If a word like *free* is essential to your message, use *fr*ee* to avoid being incorrectly filtered, but be careful not to overuse the asterisk.

- Avoid excessive use of "click here."

- Avoid use of multiple exclamation points (!!!!) or question marks (????). Not only is that perceived as condescending, many spam filters trip on improper or overused punctuation.

- Avoid using *$$* and other symbols normally not used in standard communications.

5. Did you know most e-mail programs can be set to not download e-mails that are over a certain size and can be automatically deleted without being downloaded? Do not embed graphics within your e-mail or send large attachments without notice. Ask first before you send so that the party is waiting for your e-mail and it won't be deleted off the server without downloading.

6. Refrain from formatting your e-mails. If not done properly, formatting can cause your e-mails to be identified as spam. Get used to getting your message across in a clear and concise manner by choosing the proper verbiage, sentence structure, and grammar.

When using any sort of spam software or filtering system, before you purge your trash, it doesn't hurt to do a quick peak to see if any e-mails are in fact from folks you know or recognize who do not follow the above guidelines and are mistakenly identified as spammy.

ALL ABOUT VIRUSES

For years I have been advising folks that they really "should" keep on top of the virus scene if for no other reason than to save them the grief a subsequent virus infection can cause. Those days are way over. You no longer have a choice on this topic; you need to make sure if you are going to participate online that you take the responsibility to ensure the necessary practices are in place to keep your system and those you communicate with as risk free as possible from infection.

When you hear about million-dollar losses due to the latest virus "attack," know that the only way a virus can "attack" is if (a) you let it by not being responsible, or (b) you refuse to become informed on this subject and therefore you let the virus in to wreck havoc on your system as well as the systems of those you communicate with. There is no faster way to look silly and uninformed than to have all your business associates receive multiple virus-generated e-mails sending them to a pornography site generated from your e-mail account. (Can we say *grovel*?)

Virus protection is relatively simple with some basic knowledge and software, both on the server/network side and the user side. My concern is with the user side and to stress to each of you the importance of protecting your system from potential destructive viruses. Protecting yourself, your computer, and those you communicate with is a responsibility of participation, not a choice.

Over are the days of having to click on an attachment link for the virus to propagate and for you to get infected. That ended with the virus W32.Nimda.A@mm in September 2001 that merely required you click on the subject of the e-mail in your e-mail program (specifically targeting Outlook users)—you didn't even have to open the message itself. Nimda then followed and also propagated itself by taking advantage of bugs in servers to plant itself on certain servers and then transfer itself to those who visited the Web sites on that server.

The days of pretending you have no control and are an innocent victim has come to an end. You need to use products that cannot be compromised if at all possible, but you also need to have 24/7 virus software running on your system and then update your virus patterns daily. Yes, daily or, if you are not online every day, each time you log on!

Networks and servers with experienced, astute IT staffs did not get infected by Nimda—they kept abreast of their products and downloaded the latest patches both for their servers and company's browsers before problems could arise. Those who create viruses target the masses—Outlook users for example—as they know they are the majority, less tech savvy, and less prone to take precautions to stop their efforts.

Why all the fuss? Well, I personally think viruses up to now have been "fun and games" compared to what they could do or will do in the near future. Nimda was an example of this. As in wipe out hard drives, extrapolate personal data, engage malicious code, or plant code on your computer. When that happens, you will experience the very same feeling those who don't back up their computers do when they have lost all their data in a hard-drive crash. If they had only taken those few simple steps to avoid the pain and misery . . . as they say, hindsight is 20/20.

Another important concern is those of us who do practice

technology safely really get frustrated receiving all the e-mails these viruses create from others who don't bother to take these simple steps. If everyone followed these basic steps, those who create these viruses wouldn't have it so darned easy! It is a tremendous waste of time and resources that can be avoided. So if you don't have software that protects your computer from the moment you boot up as well as real-time e-mail scanning as you download e-mail, put down this book and go download virus software now!

For your information: the basics of viruses.

- **What is a computer virus?** A computer virus is a program designed to spread itself by first infecting executable files or the system areas of hard and floppy disks and then making copies of itself. Viruses usually operate without the knowledge or desire of the computer user.

- **What kind of files can spread viruses?** Viruses have the potential to infect any type of executable code, not just the files that are commonly called "program files." For example, some viruses infect executable code in the boot sector of floppy disks or in system areas of hard drives. Another type of virus, known as a "macro" virus, can infect word-processing and spreadsheet documents that use macros—such as Word for Windows. And it's possible, although highly improbable on legitimate business sites, for HTML documents containing JavaScript or other types of executable code to spread viruses or other malicious code.

  Since virus code must be executed to have any effect, files that the computer treats as pure data are safe. This includes graphics and sound files such as *.gif*, *.jpg*, *.mp3*, *.wav*, etc., as well as plain text in *.txt* files.

For example, just viewing picture files won't infect your computer with a virus. The virus code has to be in a form, such as an .exe program file or a Word .doc file, which the computer will actually try to execute by opening a program.

- **How do viruses spread?** When you execute program code that's infected by a virus, the virus code will run and try to infect other programs, either on the same computer or on other computers connected to it over a network. And the newly infected programs will try to infect yet more programs and so on and so forth. When you share a copy of an infected file with other computer users, running the file may also infect their computers; and files from those computers may spread the infection to yet more computers. And so on and so forth.

  If your computer is infected with a boot-sector virus, the virus tries to write copies of itself to the system areas of floppy disks and hard disks. Then the infected floppy disks may infect other computers that boot from them, and the virus copy on the hard disk will try to infect still more floppies. Some viruses, known as "multipartite" viruses, can spread both by infecting files and by infecting the boot areas of floppy disks.

- **What do viruses do to computers?** Viruses are software programs, and they can do the same things as any other programs running on a computer. The actual effect of any particular virus depends on how it was programmed by the person who wrote the virus. Some viruses are deliberately designed to damage files or otherwise interfere with your computer's operation, while others don't do anything but try to spread themselves around and be a nuisance. But even those that just spread themselves are harmful, since they damage files and may cause other problems during the process of spreading. Note that viruses can't do any damage to hardware: they won't melt down your CPU, burn out your hard drive, cause your monitor to explode, etc. Warnings about viruses that will physically destroy your computer are usually hoaxes and are not legitimate virus warnings.

- **What is a Trojan Horse program?** A type of program that is often confused with viruses is a "Trojan Horse" program. This is not a virus, but simply a program (often harmful) that pretends to be something else. For example, you might download what you think is a new program; but when you run it, it deletes files on your hard drive. Or the third time you start the program, the program e-mails your saved passwords to another person.

  Note: simply downloading a file to your computer won't activate a virus or Trojan Horse; you have to execute the code in the file to trigger it. This could mean running a program file or opening a Word/Excel document that can execute any macros within the document.

- **What's the story on viruses and e-mail?** You can't get a virus just by reading a plain-text e-mail message. What you have to watch out for are encoded messages containing embedded executable code (i.e., JavaScript in an HTML message) or messages that include an executable file attachment (i.e., an encoded program file or a Word document containing macros). In order to activate a virus or Trojan Horse program, your computer has to execute some type of code. This could be a program attached to an e-mail, a Word document you downloaded from the Internet, or something received on a CD or floppy disk.

- **What can I do to reduce the chance of getting viruses from e-mail?** Have real-time, 24/7 virus protection and update your virus patterns minimally every time you log on! I update my software overnight and each afternoon to make sure I am covered from the latest virus releases. Treat any file attachments that might contain executable code as carefully as you would any other new files: save the attachment to disk and then check it with an up-to-date virus scanner before opening the file if you do not have real-time protection.

If your e-mail software has the ability to automatically execute JavaScript, Word macros, or other executable code contained in or attached to a message, I strongly recommend that you disable this feature.

If an executable file shows up unexpectedly attached to an e-mail, you should delete it unless you can positively verify what it is, whom it came from, and why it was sent to you—and even then still scan it with your software to make sure it is safe. The Melissa virus was a dramatic demonstration of the need to be extremely careful when you receive e-mail with attached files or documents. Just because an e-mail appears to come from someone you trust, this does not mean the file is safe or that the supposed sender had anything to do with it.

Remember what I mentioned above about those who don't back up their data? Do regular backups. Some viruses and Trojan Horse programs will erase or corrupt files on your hard drive, and a recent backup may be the only way to recover your data. Ideally, you should back up your entire system on a regular basis. Say once a week or at the end of every Friday. If this isn't practical, at least backup the files that you can't afford to lose or that would be difficult to replace such as critical business and accounting files, documents, bookmark files, address books, important e-mail, etc.

There you have it in a nutshell. You can't nor should you as a responsible Netizen ignore this information. It is your responsibility to absorb and apply it, or you could risk not only your data, but time, money, as well as friends, family, and potential customers who will not be too pleased about your lack of attention to this subject when you pass your irresponsibility on to them.

TO E-CARD OR
NOT TO E-CARD

Each holiday season, I get e-mail asking if sending e-greetings or e-cards in lieu of hard-copy traditional holiday cards through standard snail mail is acceptable. I also get requests throughout the year about the appropriateness of using e-cards in lieu of traditional hard-copy cards sent through snail mail for weddings, birthdays, and even, yes, condolences.

One thing I have learned in all my years online is that "acceptable" is definitely subjective. I look at it this way—thoughtful is as thoughtful does. Personally, I prefer to send actual cards in envelopes by way of Uncle Sam's snail mail. You remember those, don't you? You can open the envelopes after looking at the return address label to see whom they are from. You can touch and feel them as you open to view that special message with actual signatures and hang them up as part of your Holiday decorations as I do each year. You cannot hang up e-cards—well you could by printing them, but it just wouldn't be the same.

I guess it all depends on how you view the various holidays combined with your personal definition of what acceptable is to you. I am of the seemingly old-fashioned belief that there is a time and place for quickie e-cards—certain holidays or condolences not being one of them. I prefer to pick holiday and special occasion cards out myself, sign and address each one by hand. As I do each year, I send out hand-addressed and signed holiday cards that require postage. Thoughtful is as thoughtful does.

E-greetings are more appropriate for those that you only have an electronic or virtual relationship with. For those types of relationships, e-cards are perfectly apropos. They are not very personal; they do not cost anything in money or time, taking only a moment to input an e-mail address and click send. With e-cards, in general, if you find a nifty e-card that makes you think of a specific person you would like to send it to, then go ahead. Most likely they will certainly appreciate the thought because they will know why you choose that particular card for them. If is it unique and fun and something you know they will enjoy, send away! You know what I mean . . . you see the card and immediately think of that individual because either the content or visuals of the e-card makes you think of them—specifically.

If the e-card is not that personal or if you have an established off-line relationship with the individual in question, don't those you care about deserve more then a generic greeting sent via e-mail? Just because technology makes so much, so much easier doesn't mean we take shortcuts every chance we get, does it? Nothing like getting that card on a special occasion knowing you meant enough to the sender for them to pick the card especially for you and go through the time, effort, and cost to send it your way. It speaks volumes to the recipient when you go out to a store and find that special card that lets the other person know that you are thinking of them. You picked it out, you paid for it—you paid for the postage, handwrote the envelope and inside greeting, and sent it off in time to them for that occasion. Now that is truly thoughtful!

Nowadays, rare are the envelopes with handwritten addresses to be opened to find personally signed heart felt wishes reflecting the true meaning of most holidays. It is all too common to receive cards with address labels noting the recipient's address enclosing greetings with preprinted names inside—not a personal handwritten touch to be found! I guess those could be the same folks who would find e-cards acceptable for condolences. Everyone has to do what works for them. For me, I didn't send a single holiday e-card and don't plan on it in the future. Just know that whatever you do and how you do it from birthday greetings, to condolences, to the holidays, your choice of actions will reflect on your priorities and what is important to you based on the time you were willing to spend. One thing I am sure you'll agree, there is nothing like getting an old-fashioned card addressed to you in your mailbox with a handwritten, heartfelt greeting within. Thoughtful is as thoughtful does.

DOMAIN SLAMMING

If you do not yet own a domain name, you may one day. For those who do own domains in current use or for future endeavors, you have undoubtedly received e-mails or notices in your snail mail about your domain expiring. Sometimes months or, in some cases, years in advance of the actual renewal date. When it comes to domains, there is big business taking advantage of what you don't know—just as with most e-mail spam. Many times simply taking advantage of what you won't take the time to read. We're all rushed—not enough time in every day. Daily I hear folks who exclaim "Too much information!" when it comes to technology. That is the biggest challenge of all—for each of us—to determine what information you need to rely on, pay attention to, or the majority of times to simply ignore.

When it comes to your domain name(s), this is a topic you need to pay attention to. This is where having a technology partner you can rely on to give you the straight scoop is also invaluable. Not the scoop that makes them the most money, not the scoop they "think" may work or "heard" about—the scoop that is important to you and your online collateral.

Remember a while back when telephone companies were accused of "slamming" customers by either calling them in the guise of a customer service agent for their current provider or sending out $25 checks that you could cash? I still see these checks on occasion; they're now up to $40. By providing your account info to these "customer service" agents or cashing that check, you were inadvertently switching your carrier without a clear and concise explanation that was in fact what you were doing. Well, if you read the fine print . . . but who does that? Domain slammers also count on you to not read the fine print. And to their later regret, many domain owners do not read that fine print.

This type of methodology has now made its way into the online arena. Say hello to "domain slamming." A different company appears almost weekly pulling similar tactics. Some send "expiration notices" or "renewals" by snail mail or e-mail giving the perception that they are the company you have your domains registered with—which isn't the case. What you don't know or read will be used to get you to unknowingly transfer your domain. Do you want to work with a company that relies on this type of methodology to gain new customers? I think not.

Not to defend these tactics, but . . . the devil is in the details. These companies do state the reality of their offer in the fine print. If you don't read the print, then who is at fault? Both sides! The registrar using these tactics tailors a notice that looks as though it is an expiration notice counting on you to not read the fine print and/or that you don't know or remember where you registered your domain. And they count on that. The registrant, you the domain owner, who doesn't read the fine print and just assumes or doesn't verify the offer, is also at fault. Believe it or not, it is quite common for me to run into those who have relied on others for their domain registration efforts and either didn't care or make an effort to note who the registrar is.

So let's see how we can avoid this situation from the domain owner's point of view by educating you on a couple issues in regard to domain renewals and transfers in general, so when you receive this type of e-mail or snail mail you are informed:

Registrar: a company in the business of offering domain name services. Reputable companies are accredited by ICANN—the Internet Corporation for Assigned Names and Numbers. You can check to see if a registrar is accredited by going to their Web site at: http://www.icann.org, and I do not recommend working with any company that does not have this accreditation. You can file a complaint as an FYI with this organization for companies that you have issues with. ICANN will not resolve the situation for you, but they do track trends and may take action if enough users complain. Registrars can obtain ownership of domains where annual renewal fees are in arrears or they can choose to make the domain available to the public. Read the fine print specific to the terms for each registrar.

Registrant is the actual owner of the domain—you. I hope. I run into Netizens all the time that had some "Web designer" register their domain for them. The Web designer's name is down on the record as the registrant—in effect, meaning the Web designer officially owns your domain. If this is the case for you, you need to have your name and contact information formally changed to reflect as the registrant on your domain record. If a domain's ownership changes, the registrant's approval will be required in writing and notarized (sans not paying your annual fees). If you are not down as the registrant for your domain, legally you are not the owner—the individual/company listed is, and you will need to work with them, immediately, to get this information corrected.

Administrative Contact is generally the individual who knows the domain system well enough to make changes to the record if need be. They can be the registrant; however, most registrants do not understand the process well enough to be their own administrative contact. This is where having a consultant you can trust as your administrative contact is recommended.

Technical Contact is generally the individual/company responsible for the domain-name servers where your domain is stored or hosted.

Billing Contact is generally the entity that will be contacted for renewal and billing issues. With some hosting companies who are also registrars, they may handle the renewal of your domains automatically and bill you on your next hosting invoice therefore they are down as the billing contact.

Changes. Domain registrars require a confirmation, usually by e-mail, from an individual already on the domain's record who is authorized to make any changes to a domain record before a change/transfer can be formalized and processed. Change of registrant is required in writing.

Transfers. To successfully transfer your domains to another registrar, you should plan on initiating your request within at least a thirty-day window previous to the actual renewal/expiration date of your domain to be successful. This allows enough time for the confirmation e-mail process to be completed or repeated if e-mails are not received or inadvertently trashed. Some registrars have a "lock-out" date that any requests made under that window will not be honored.

Now that we have some of the verbiage out of the way, let's get to the crux of this matter. Domain slamming. Some of the top registrars have been known to send out "renewal" letters to registrants that originally registered their domains with other registrars stating that their domain is up for renewal hoping they inadvertently transfer their domain to their service. The more astute registrars have backed off these practices due to widespread complaints claiming deceptive practices. At almost any credible registrar, you can find a message to their customers warning them to not assume renewal letters or e-mails are from their original registrar. This is where knowing where you or your consultant registered your domains and who your domain registrar is, is critical. The attention getter with these "renewal letters" is that they are many times offering a less expensive fee to entice you. Many times only offering long multi-year commitments to experience the savings offered. This is certainly an instance, amongst many others online, where shopping on price alone may not be the best deal.

What happens? Domain owners do not realize that the letter is not from the company they originally registered with, and therefore "renew" when in reality they end up unknowingly transferring their domain. If someone unfamiliar with domain renewals/transfers begins this process, you could cause your Web site to go off-line or worse yet; lose ownership of your domain(s).

If you receive an "Important Notice" or "Domain Expiration Notice" from any registrar who is not the one you originally registered your domain(s) with, simply throw it away. Regardless of their claims of you missing an opportunity or having to spend more money later, ignore them. Their "notices" are created to give you the impression that they are the original registrars offering you a deal. You send your check, confirm by e-mail, and your domain gets transferred to them and you are then their customer. Worse yet, if you realize the error you made, just try to get them to provide a refund or resolve the situation in a friendly and professional tone. Based on my experience, that won't happen.

One simple step to take to avoid any problems in regard to your domain collateral is to immediately contact your technology consultant to verify if in fact the communication (postal mail, e-mail, or phone) is legit and to get their recommendations. Unless the communication is from the company you originally registered your domain name with and you know that for a fact, most likely the communication is nothing more than a sales letter trying to entice you away.

Most domain record information is publicly available at domain registrars in their Search or "Whois" feature. There is no reason for you to not know where your domain was registered or who is on your contact information. You should verify your contact information and update it regularly to ensure it reflects your accurate and current information in case any issues arise. You can verify who your Registrar is as well as your contact and actual expiration dates at my "Do It Yourself" site: http://www.theistudio.net. Click in "Whois" at the bottom of the page to search the database.

Every registrar has its own "whois" database. The above is simply one of many and a way for those of you who were not aware of the details in this chapter to get the ball rolling.

Protect yourself from companies that will assume you will not double-check their claims. Take the time to note and document where your domains are registered right now if you have not already. Get a piece of paper out right now, and for each domain name you own, write down where you registered it and when it expires so you have that information readily available when these "notices" arrive.

As with anything, always read the fine print. Because, as you know, with information technology, information is power, but only if you use it!

TAKE THE TECHNOLOGY CHALLENGE

Being proudly self-employed, I often think about what a great country I live in overflowing with opportunities everywhere I look.

Wealth is the product of man's capacity to think.
—Ayn Rand

The United States of America, unlike any other, gives its citizens the opportunity to become whatever they choose to be—or not be for that matter. But make no mistake, you do choose what you make of yourself—personally or in business. You do have control over what you can or will accomplish. Based on your choices, your work ethic, and how you live your life. Technology affects lives differently—individually—based on each person's chosen set of attitudes and perceptions. You choose the attitude you will have; you choose the information you seek (or do not seek) to base your perceptions on. You have the freedom to make those choices. There are tons of people in other countries who would use that freedom of choice to its full potential had they that option available to them, but they don't.

The last of the human freedoms
is to choose one's attitudes.
—Victor Frankl

The addition of technology to the "American dream's" recipe really makes becoming successful and attaining that "piece of the pie" within the grasp of every person who has the desire and commitment to just reach out and grab it. Literally! Never at any time in our history are there so many opportunities available for each individual so inclined to succeed. Technology has broken down the barriers and made information, education, and resources available to those who merely started with the desire to seek it out. What freedom of knowledge! No longer can one sit back and say they "can't" get involved in technology. If someone isn't involved, for the most part it is because they don't want to be out of fear, intimidation, frustration, laziness, or just plain old lack of interest. And they have the freedom to make that choice.

Even those who do not yet own their own computer have the local library with computers where they can get online to access the rich wealth of information that makes the "dream" within reach. Cyber/Internet cafes are popping up in even the smallest rural towns. If there is a will, there is a way! Why then with all this opportunity are so many unable or unwilling to take advantage of it? While we all "want" to own our home, financial independence, and our share of expensive toys, why are so few open to making the choices and sacrifices necessary to make their dreams a reality? Attitudes (I can't, I won't, I don't want to, I shouldn't have to) and perceptions (it's too difficult, too expensive, too time consuming, too challenging). Could it be lack of work ethic or lack of education? Or is it lack of personal commitment or unwillingness to work for something worth having?

> Liberty means responsibility.
> That is why most men dread it.
> —George Bernard Shaw

I don't believe that the majority of those in this or other countries actually believe that technology is a "right" or should hand them opportunity or success on a silver platter. Have we really become that spoiled that we are no longer willing to work for our dreams no matter what that entails? Especially with technology making the "dream" easier than ever, more accessible than before, and more available to many with more opportunity than most know what to do with!

I find that the harder I work, the more luck I seem to have.
—Thomas Jefferson

If you were to interview any of our country's founders about how easy many today think success should be, what little effort should be necessary, what little investment one would prefer to make to reach unrealistic goals, you would likely be put in shackles in the local jail house until you were thinking straight! You most probably would have been laughed at by the likes of Washington, Jefferson, and Lincoln for having such silly thoughts, because they knew anything worth having, that you believe in, is worth unending commitment and sacrifice. Why should technological success be any different? You have the freedom to make these choices.

What I think our predecessors would find surprising is how few are up to the challenge of using technology to make their dreams come to fruition. They would scoff at the fact that people were unwilling to acquire the necessary knowledge and skills to succeed because it takes too much time or work. They would gasp at the thought that many believe any goal worth pursuing should have no cost or responsibility involved. If they were here today, they likely would be disappointed and probably insulted that a chunk of current citizens of this fine country which they helped build with their ideals and sacrifices would actually prefer to believe that everything is a right, everything is a given, whatever one wants should just happen without effort, accountability, sacrifice, or commitment.

Only those who dare to fail greatly
can ever achieve greatly.
—Robert Francis Kennedy

They would quickly point out that to reach ones goals you have to work harder than you ever thought, sacrifice more than you could imagine, invest as necessary to reach those goals—do what is right! Only those that do will reach their goals. Technology is opportunity for those with the freedom to choose what to do with it, those who will work at it, those who will learn and invest and learn some more. They will succeed. The rest, well they'll just be on the sidelines—and they have the freedom to make that choice.

I do not think much of a man who is not wiser today than he was yesterday.
—Abraham Lincoln

With technology, every day is an opportunity where one can improve their lives. Entrepreneurs and businesses of all sizes have the ability to communicate and connect with vendors, customers, and markets that even a few years ago were impossible. Moms and dads, grandmoms and grandpops are all connecting and getting online to access information that enriches their personal lives. From hobbies to discussion groups, learning about technology, and gaining the necessary skills is opening up new worlds to millions. But there is only one road to travel.

Success seems to be largely a matter of hanging on after others have let go.
—William Feather

By doing things the right way (which may not necessarily the easy way or "your" way), investing as needed and acquiring the necessary skills and knowledge, the sky really is the limit, personally and professionally. For example, I know that if someone partners with my company and has the sincere desire and commitment to succeed with technology, I can take them there. I give each new client my personal guarantee in that regard. But they have to make the right efforts in the right areas based on the reality of what is necessary in order to lay the groundwork for that success which then produces financial freedom—part of the American dream we all strive for. Are you up to this challenge?

> Many an opportunity is lost because
> a man is out looking for four-leaf clovers.
> —Anonymous

Take the Technology Challenge to see if you have what it takes to make technology your stairway to success. Technology is not for the weak of heart nor is it easy. Rate each question based on a 1-10 scale, with 10 being you agree with the statement 100 percent.

- Without spending the required time learning and practicing the skills necessary to use technology properly, my chances to enjoy technology and succeed are extremely diminished.

- Knowledge acquisition will be an ongoing challenge to keep up with technology as it evolves, and I am prepared to be on a continual learning curve and tackle the frustrations that will bring.

- There are an established set of unwritten rules and guidelines which are part of the Internet "culture," which is a self-governing society. I will need to be aware of and practice these guidelines in order to be most effective and perceived as favorably as possible by those I communicate with.

- An ongoing program implementing the basics of running an organized and successful business is important to my level of commercial success with technology. The basics of knowing how to use my computer, e-mail program, and browser are important to me understanding technology's capabilities for personal fulfillment and enjoyment.

- With very little to limited knowledge about technology, in general, I realize I need to choose my resources, mentors, and partners carefully so I have proven experience on my team to trust and rely on for the best possible experience. This requires I not choose partners solely on price alone, claims of ease of use, or instant results.

- Technology is evolving daily, requiring ongoing updates, changes, and new directions that I will need to embrace and implement on a consistent basis in order to keep in step with technology and if online for business, in front of my competitors.

- Information technology means that I will need to review all data and information available and provided to me on a regular basis in order to truly understand where I am coming from and where I will need to go to accomplish my goals.

- If I want to have a successful online enterprise, one to three hours online minimally per day will be necessary for me to answer e-mail, network, market, and organize my online activities and opportunities. If online for personal enjoyment, the courteous thing to do is check e-mail regularly and respond properly and promptly.

- Online success is there for the taking if I make the right choices, efforts, and commitment. This includes realizing that success doesn't just happen—I need to work at it, possibly harder than anything I've ever worked at before to make it happen!

- An open mind and a small ego are imperative in order to be able to embrace the ideas and information, the recommendations, and advice given by those with the experience to help me reach my goals. To override relevant data, recommendations, or advice based on my very limited knowledge, without any other solid reason to do so, will hinder my enjoyment and potential success.

Anywhere you gave a less than 10 will indicate where you may not be up to the challenge or have unrealistic expectations of what technology will demand of you to participate. That doesn't mean you can't get there—it just means you need a bit of reality check before you begin.

Technology doesn't wait or mollycoddle anyone—no matter how techno-challenged you may be. Some try to kid themselves either based on stories from friends or hype on some Web site that the above level of effort and knowledge are not required. They have the freedom to believe what they want; they have the freedom to make their own choices.

Wouldn't you rather use your freedom of choice to seek out the reality of how to use technology and then make it yours? Technology is a challenge for everyone who plays—even those of us who participate for a living are challenged on almost a daily basis with some new concept, trend, or data that surprises and many times perplexes us which demands we react, rethink, and redo. Realize that online nothing is a right or a given or written in stone.

There are no shortcuts to any place worth going.
—Anonymous

If you want to play and succeed, there are things you will need to learn, hills you will need to climb, and decisions you will need to make. It won't just happen—you need to make it happen. You have the freedom to make these choices. Use your freedom to make the choice to use technology properly, to do what it takes, to rise to the challenge! Isn't it time you stepped up to the plate and claimed your right to succeed and use your freedom to learn, your independence to make your own choices and stand by them until you reach your goals?

We are told never to cross a bridge until we come to it, but this world is owned by men who have "crossed bridges" in their imagination far ahead of the crowd.
—Anonymous

So stand up straight! Shoulders back! Get that complacent look off your face and change your attitude! Technology (as with life) isn't easy—nor is it cheap in time or for commercial gain, expense! But then, neither is success. What do you think our founding fathers would do given the opportunity such as you have right now?

SOMETHING'S PHISHY

Many onliners have contacted me frustrated with the type of e-mail requests they are receiving that have to do with asking for personal information and how would one know if the e-mail is legit or not. Being an avid eBayer and PayPal.com user, I have received "spoofed" e-mails from someone out there asking me to update or confirm personal information for both accounts, including my SS number and credit card numbers!

These e-mails "looked" official—had the correct logos and even what appeared to be valid dot-coms to click on to go and complete a form asking for all my information. I knew how to determine these e-mail were not legit and sent a copy of each to both eBay and PayPal so they were aware that someone was "spoofing" their identity to get their customer's sensitive personal information. Many times this type of information gathering is what leads to identity fraud. Here is how it works and how you can avoid being misled.

What these scambos do is take the logos right off the site they want to spoof. Being you can right click and then "save as" pretty much anything online, that isn't too hard to accomplish. Then within the e-mail, they code in those graphics so the e-mail looks as though it is coming from the site they want you to believe is contacting you.

The URL or Web address you need to click on to go to their Web site and update or renew your information can look authentic. However, buried within the HTML code of that very e-mail, you are being sent to a phony site that has nothing to do with the company it appears is asking you to update or confirm your information—such as an eBay or PayPal—or even your financial institution.

This type of scam is known as "phishing." Add another wacky word to your online vocabulary! Phishing is a scam that uses spam to deceive consumers into disclosing their personal information. First phishers steal a company's identity by spoofing their look using logos stolen from the original sites, and then they use it to mislead consumers so they can steal their credit identities.

Here are some tips to avoid being a phish and getting hooked:

- If you receive an e-mail that warns you, with little to no notice, that an account of yours will be shut down unless you reconfirm your billing information by clicking on a link within the e-mail to go to a Web site, do not reply or click on the link in the e-mail. Another tactic is to claim their database crashed and they need you to resubmit your info—don't believe it!

- Instead, contact the company referenced in the e-mail using a telephone number or through their Web site you know to be genuine or that you have bookmarked to your favorites. Many times the genuine sites being spoofed have actual account logins where you can go and confirm your information. If these e-mails come from a site you login to on a regular basis and know that you have the option to update your own information there at any time, be very leery of any e-mail that does anything other than request that you login as usual to update or confirm your information through your normal procedures.

- Never ever provide or send personal and financial information by e-mail. I have worked with clients who have e-mailed me their credit card numbers because they trust me. That's all fine and I am grateful for their trust, but what if they typo my e-mail address and it goes to the wrong party or worse yet what if that e-mail is farmed in-between point A and point B by someone looking for just an opportunity to get hold of someone's credit card info?

- If you are sent to a Web site, be sure you see the familiar dot-com you are used to seeing in the location bar of your browser once you are there. Using eBay and PayPal as examples, only ebay.com or paypal.com should be in the Web site address field at the top of your browser window to be authentic. To give you some examples:

OK: http://updates.ebay.com

Only eBay, the owner of ebay.com has the ability to add any subsites *before* their main domain name ebay.com such as "updates" above.

Not OK: http://ebay.anotherdomain.com (example only)

The scammer owning "anotherdomain.com" can add any company name it wants on the server side before their domain name to give you the perception of legitimacy.

Definitely not OK: 206.254.123.23 (IP number—example only)

If you see an IP number only—no dot anything—run! In this instance, this would be considered a throw-away site that is ready to go off-line and disappear because they haven't even bothered to get a domain name to identify themselves by.

• If you have determined the Web site to be legitimate and do decide to submit financial information, look for the "lock" icon in the lower right-hand corner on the browser's bottom status bar and for an address that starts with https: both of which signal that your information is secure and encrypted during transmission. Do not submit information without *both* of these visuals in place.

• Each month, take the time to review your credit card and bank account statements as soon as you receive them to determine whether there are any unauthorized activities. If your statement is late by more than a couple of days, call your credit card company or bank to confirm your billing address and account balances.

• If you believe you have been scammed, report the suspicious activity to the Federal Trade Commission at http://www.ftc.gov.

The bottom line is to double-check any e-mails that request personal information by going to the site you have bookmarked or by calling them on the old-fashioned telephone to confirm. These simple efforts can help you avoid becoming a victim of identity-theft phishing.

HTML E-MAIL AND YOUR PRIVACY

Did you know? HTML e-mail allows the inclusion of graphics stored on a remote server so that when you open the e-mail, the graphic is loaded and lets the sender know:

- you've opened the message. Sort of a stealth version of a Return Receipt.

- you have a valid e-mail message because you opened the e-mail—therefore allowing it to be resold to spammers.

- your current IP address. Hackers can exploit this as the remote image is a way to retrieve IP addresses for dial-up accounts that receive a different IP every time they log in.

- If your e-mail client uses Internet Explorer or Netscape to display HTML e-mails, the sender of an e-mail message can set a cookie in your browser and thus identify you the next time you visit their site.

Just think about how many junk e-mails you have received with formatting or that appear blank. Bingo—the above could have just happened to you!

What can you do about this?

- Look at the **From** and **Subject** field of all incoming e-mail. If you do not know the sender and the subject does not make sense, hit Delete before opening the e-mail. If you don't open the e-mail, the request cannot be sent to the remote server.

- Request all newsletters or informational e-mail be sent as plain text if given the option. Unfortunately, sometimes overzealous marketers can't help themselves!

- Read all e-mail, especially HTML e-mail off-line. You won't know it is HTML until you open it and the damage is done. Download your e-mail, get off-line, and then review your new messages. This way your activities cannot be reported to a remote server if you are not online.

- Configure your e-mail program to turn off HTML display. That works for all but Microsoft Outlook. (Ever wonder why Outlook users suffer most when new viruses come out?) Outlook users should set their e-mail security zone to "Trusted Sites" (Security tab in Options menu) and then turn off cookies for this zone in Internet Explorer. This will not allow sites you access from your e-mail client to set cookies. This is a bit extreme but the only way in Outlook to prevent HTML e-mail spies. Rather than block all URLs from those in plain text or that are legitimate, you can simply cut-and-paste site addresses into your browser.

I don't know about you, but I care not to have those who send me e-mail, especially spammers, know when I opened it, what my IP address is, or to set cookies via HTML e-mail. That said, not all cookies are bad. Be sure to read the next chapter, "Cookies—No Fat, Zero Calories?" Servers use cookies

to track unique visitors while not gathering any specific identifiable info about you and these cookies are benign. In general, cookies are a good thing—but not when used in a manner that is specific to you without your knowledge.

I use Eudora Pro, which has a setting to prevent this type of
sneaky information gathering. Eudora allows me to unselect
"automatically download HTML graphics." Phew!

COOKIES—NO FAT, ZERO CALORIES?

In the last chapter, I brought to your attention the issues of concern with HTML e-mail. Discussed was the potential of clicking on a URL within an e-mail only to then be brought to a site that unknowing to you sets a "cookie." Since there are many misconceptions about cookies, let's get educated!

You've probably heard about cookies before. More times than not, they are described as malicious, stealth information gathering, and downright bad. This is not necessarily the case. Cookies have many positive uses as well. Such as remembering you by name at your favorite sites, or making recommendations based on previous purchases such as what is done at one of my favorite sites, Amazon.com. I love that!

First off, for those who are asking "what the heck are cookies—and what flavors do they come in?" Cookies are pieces of information generated by a Web server and stored in the user's computer, ready for future access. Generally they are very small little files placed in your browser's directory. And yes, I guess you could say they come in different flavors—but not chocolate chip or oatmeal raisin, my personal favorite.

Cookies are embedded in the HTML information flowing back and forth between a user's computer and Web site servers. Cookies allow Web sites to know it is you upon your return. They allow you to customize your experience and to save your preferences. Sites that allow you to have them remember your login information accomplish this by using cookies.

More times than not, cookies simply are tracking basic system information—type of computer, OS, time of day, general geographic location, connectivity. Not who you are via personally identifiable information such as name, sex, address etc. Nor can they arbitrarily write to other areas of your hard drive. So based on this information alone, cookies are not dangerous.

On my consulting site, in my privacy statement amongst other issues, I state in part:

> I use cookies on this site. A cookie is a piece of data stored on a site visitor's hard drive to help me improve your access to my site and identify repeat visitors to my site. Cookies can also enable me to track and target the interests of my users to enhance their experience on my site. Usage of a cookie is in no way linked to any personally identifiable information.

Now, if you fill out a form on any Web site and provide personal information, the site in question now has that information to do with it what they may. You have provided it willingly and the site is then free to store the information in its database and use it as they state based on their published privacy statement. If they do not have a privacy statement, many times they are selling your information without your knowledge—which can be much worse than most cookies.

Always seek out a site's privacy policy statement to know where they stand on what they will do with your information. Understand there are no laws or formal policing of sites in regard to how or if they follow their own privacy policies. They can say what they want and not back it up. It is up to you to decide which sites are credible, of value, and deserve your trust enough to give them any information about yourself. It behooves you to be very discerning when deciding whom you want to communicate with online—for personal or business reasons.

Many will make a big deal over the fact that these cookies are transferred and placed on your computer without your knowledge. That doesn't have to be the case if you make an effort to understand your browser software options which allow you to:

1. Disable Cookies. No cookies allowed whatsoever which is not recommended.

2. Enable Cookies for the Originating Web Site Only. This means only cookies from the site you are at can be set. Not cookies from advertisers on that site also known as third-party cookies.

3. Enable all Cookies Option. Warn me before accepting cookies. This option lets you review cookies and accept or decline them before they are set.

No. 2 above is your best choice as it allows cookies only for the sites you frequent but prevents their advertisers or partners from placing third-party cookies on your system. That happens a lot! I think you would be surprised at the number of third-party cookies currently on your system. Don't worry though; the only harm is taking up minuscule space on your hard drive.

By default, your preferences are set to allow all sites to use all cookies with no warning given when a cookie is being stored. You will need to explicitly change your preference setting if that is not what you want. To have a choice in your cookie acceptance, tweak your browser to your level of comfort:

> For Internet Explorer users: Tools/Internet Options/ Privacy/Advanced Privacy Settings
>
> For Mozilla users: Tools/Options/Security/Cookies
>
> For Netscape users: Edit/Preferences/Privacy & Security
>
> For Opera: File/Preferences/Security

Enabling or disabling all cookies is both ends of extreme and not necessary. If you are concerned, check the option to be warned so that you can choose what cookies you will allow without disallowing your favorite sites from providing a more enjoyable, personalized experience for you the next time you visit.

For a more detailed overview of cookies, check out this site:

> http://computer.howstuffworks.com/cookie1.htm

After all this talk about cookies, I'm off to the cookie jar. Or better yet, I think I'll make a batch of my favorite thick and gooey oatmeal raisin cookies that are filled with fat and calories—num, num!

APPROACHING EMPLOYERS ONLINE

One simply cannot underestimate the power of perception in your online activities! Online, folks don't have eye contact, your firm handshake, your body language to determine your sincerity or credibility. They only have how you communicate, the words you use, and how you approach them to determine if you are someone they want to communicate with—or possibly hire. With so many seeking new opportunities, I have been asked on many occasions to give an overview on this subject by site visitors. So of course, it is included in this guide for you as well!

Above and beyond the issues covered on my site and in this book, all of which will contribute to a positive perception, how you approach prospective employers online can go a long way to getting that all important follow up and to stand out from the possibly hundreds or thousands of other candidates for the same position. If you are going to use technology to job hunt, you have to make sure you reflect the skill set to do so impressively or you could end up becoming excluded right out of the gate.

- Take the time to review the prospective employer's requirements in regard to submitting your resume or CV for consideration. Not doing so gives the impression of lack of attention to detail, not to mention the inability to follow instructions.

• Never send unsolicited e-mail resumes! Most sites will offer an available opportunities area on their site about jobs that are open including specific instructions on how to send your resume. I receive on average three to five resumes each day when my site clearly states "unsolicited resumes will not be considered." What type of impression do you think that makes when I get an unasked for attachment anyway? A courtesy e-mail asking if there are any opportunities and requesting permission to send your resume and who to send it to first is highly recommended in lieu of blindly sending it along.

• Send to the specified address given or provided on an employer's site for resume submissions. Don't just send to any e-mail address you find or, worse yet, send multiple copies to multiple addresses. Take the time to review the employer's site to determine the appropriate address to use. If you are not sure, pick up the phone and ask whom you should address and send your resume to.

• Send your resume only in plain text or .rtf format (rich-text format) to ensure cross platform display. By doing so, regardless of software used by the employer or recruiter, your information can be viewed. Keep your resume limited to a brief cover letter stating your interest in that specific position and a resume of no more than two pages that highlight your experience and previous job experience. You can note additional information will be provided upon request.

• Refrain from formatting with colors or adding photos or graphics to spruce your resume up.

- Do not use Return Receipt to track when/if your resume was received or opened. This can be viewed as intrusive.

- Have a friend or associate review your cover letter and resume to catch any misspellings or grammatical mistakes that you may have missed.

Here are several useful guides on how to write your resume and cover letter:

How to Write a Resume that Will Get You a Job:
http://www.learnthat.com/courses/business/resume

How to Write a Resume:
http://www.wooster.edu/career/resumehandout/write.html

Resume Tutor:
http://www1.umn.edu/ohr/ecep/resume

HOW TO SEARCH BETTER

Tips to help you find what you're looking for amongst the over four billion pages currently indexed:

- Use more than one keyword—two to three is best. Example: classic Clark Gable movies

- Be specific. Specific terms will return more targeted results. Example: movie Gone with the Wind

- Check spelling. Be sure you've spelled your search terms correctly. Use appropriate capitalization to avoid unwanted lowercase matches. Some search engines are case sensitive. Example: White House Washington DC

- Use each search engine's "advanced search" feature to refine your search and specify the number and type of results you want.

- Use quotation marks to search for exact phrases. Example: "pink depression glass" or "Mississippi real estate for sale".

- Use plus signs to require keywords. Example: +Italian shoes

- Use minus signs to exclude keywords. Example: -ladies hat

- Choose one or two of your favorite search sites and read their online Help area. This area will provide valuable information so you can search more efficiently based on their specific features.

Remember, each search site works differently. Try several search sites on the same topic and you will find different Web sites possibly not listed by the other.

NEWBIE FAQ

These questions and answers cover the basics of getting online and enjoying the experience from an informed point of view. I hope you find them useful.

What is a FAQ?
This is a common term online that you will see a lot. It stands for **F**requently **A**sked **Q**uestions. Web sites usually focus on a very specific topic or category. Before you e-mail any questions to the site owner, read the **FAQ** first to see if your question is answered there. Many sites have forms for you to fill out where you can ask questions, give comments and suggestions. Those who solicit your comments are seriously interested in what you have to say. If you want to let them know your opinion, only do so in a constructive and polite manner after you have reviewed the site, FAQ, and other information provided. Make sure you have toured the site enough to be in a position to offer suggestions. Don't e-mail "The Ultimate CDROM Site" that you feel they should also cover sheet music. Most likely there is a sheet music site out there—go find it. That is the beauty of the Web! Don't expect every site to be the complete and total resource based on your predefined expectations.

What is Netiquette?
Netiquette is the online equivalent to off-line etiquette. It is derived from the two words: *Net*work and Et*iquette*. It behooves you to become familiar with these guidelines in regard to the socially accepted and expected behavior online.

What is snail mail?

Snail mail is the online term for old-fashioned mail sent by Uncle Sam's US Postal Service. I get a kick out of that one!

What is an ISP and how do I find one?

ISP stands for Internet service provider. You need one to connect to the Internet. For dial-up service, you want to have a local provider as geographically close to your home as possible— most consider over eight miles a toll call, so to save money make sure your connection number is no more than eight miles from your home. Always double-check with your phone company to confirm your connection number is local before you sign up for a service. $19.95-24.95 unlimited access packages do not include your telephone connection charges. For a list of ISP services, check out http://www.thelist.com where you can look for an Internet service provider by area code then prefix. If you cannot get a local call connection, check into Call Packs with your phone company.

What is the difference between an ISP and an online service like AOL?

Online services such as AOL provide their own online content, chat areas, help areas, etc. without you ever leaving their service or going out to the Internet or the actual World Wide Web; you are simply "online" with AOL. An ISP provides the phone number to call into for direct access to the actual global network and various areas of the Internet and the World Wide Web. All you need is browser software. Online services such as AOL, CompuServe, and Prodigy each provide their own type of content that is easy to find and organized to be user friendly to their customers. Online services are great starting points for newbies.

Can I use any graphics or content I find on the Web on my Web site or off-line?

No—absolutely not! Site owners take the theft of graphics, verbiage, and concepts very seriously. Most also report known offenders to their ISPs and hosting company which many times gets their accounts cancelled for the theft of copyright protected materials. Many newbies are under this impression that just because you can take a graphic or copy a page, that means it is OK. This simply is not the case! Please review the law: http://www.copyright.gov/title17, Public Law 105-147—105th Congress—"This ACT Approved December 16, 1997, provides new and stiffer penalties for anyone who infringes a copyright willfully . . . by the reproduction or distribution, including by electronic means."

What browser software should I use?
You can use any browser you prefer to use the Internet and the Web, and it behooves you to keep up with browser upgrades to take advantage of all the possibilities current technology has to offer. At this time, the most popular browser software is Microsoft Internet Explorer. There are several other browsers available that some prefer such as Mozilla, Netscape, and Opera. By using anything less than the 4.0 versions, you are limited in what you can experience at many Web sites. Even AOLers can now use their browser of choice. AOL has a comprehensive section in their help area about how to configure your settings to use the browser of your choice rather than what is included with AOL software.

What are these search engine things?
In a way, search engines are the online equivalent of the yellow pages. Put in a term and/or phrase and it will return a list of Web sites that match or are close to the criteria you requested. Each search engine, search site, or directory will serve up a different combination for the same exact search and those results will constantly change based on each service's algorithm changes. Pick a search engine that you like and learn how to use it by reading the FAQ or Support Area. By doing so, you will be a more efficient searcher and

save yourself some time and frustration. The top places to search the entire World Wide Web are Google.com, Yahoo.com, and MSN.com.

What the heck is a URL?

URL = Uniform Resource Locator. All the www.dot.dot. com.net.dot.enough.com's you see all over the place are actually URLs. When at a site that you think you may like to visit again in the future, you need to remember where it was at, you need the URL. Depending on your software you can Bookmark the site or add the site to your "Favorite Places." The software will then save the location by title for you. Remember, when copying a site's URL from the newspaper or other off-line media you need to get the URL correct—no spaces and only have dashes where noted. One space, dash, or dot where it shouldn't be and you will most likely have to use a search engine and start all over again and hope you duplicate how you found the site in the first place.

How about a couple quick e-mail tips?

1. Spell check.
2. Proof-read.
3. Never type in all caps.
4. Always be courteous.

Typing in all caps is considered screaming or yelling online, and you will get e-mails pointing this out to you. Remember, the world has only your words to judge you by. Also, if you receive an e-mail from another party (not spam), have the courtesy to respond. Honestly, all too often I am appalled at the lack of courtesy shown by those who do not bother to respond to e-mails; even if it is to thank the sender for taking the time to write. Tsk, tsk, tsk!

What is spam? I thought it was a luncheon meat.

Never, ever send e-mail to anyone who has not asked you to—especially about your business or something you can commercially gain from. Whether you send them a direct e-mail or go from site to site cutting-and-pasting your sales pitch into their Web site form—it is spam. Spam is not tolerated on the Internet. Spam is the online equivalent of the junk mail you find in your snail-mail box.

If you have been online any length of time, you have been spammed by e-mail selling you everything from get-rich opportunities to the how to lose weight. Just hit your Delete button. Yes, there is software that assists with mass e-mailing, and yes, you can buy e-mail addresses from brokers—but believe me, don't do it, don't do it! You will regret it. Your otherwise credible business could take a beating by using these types of tactics on the Internet. Take the time to learn the correct way to get the word out about your products or services by working with a seasoned professional and do it the right way! And remember . . . just as in life, if it sounds too good to be true it usually is!

I can hear you now . . . "You say not to spam, but I receive handfuls of these e-mails a day! If it works for them, why won't it work for me?" Actually, when I get asked this question, it tells me that questioner is either a newbie and/or wants to take advantage of other newbies. Not only is spamming poor Netiquette that will have a negative impact on your business's image, in some states it is now against the law. Have you ever heard of the term "wannabe"—someone "who wants to be" something they aren't? That is the likes of which you will be included with if you spam. Bottom line is, if you are credible and ethical, which many of these spammers are not, you will channel your efforts in a more appropriate acceptable direction. Many will make that comment that it "works for these companies." How do you know this to be true?

Most are just wannabes falling for a marketing scam that includes e-mailing folks to try to get them to buy something. Just because someone sends e-mail giving the perception of being a credible company (which most spammers do not make even that much effort) does not make it so—in most cases it is proportionately the opposite. Just don't do it or believe it!

I can get flamed? What is that and does it hurt?

If you spam, you will be flamed. If you are nasty, rude, or don't follow posted rules you can also get flamed. Act like a jerk, you will be flamed. You can plan on getting flamed when not practicing proper Netiquette or common courtesies. Flames are nasty e-mails from people you don't know who will tell you exactly how they feel about your lack of courtesy, comments, or practices. Does it hurt? It will hurt only your pride and reputation. Do not underestimate the potential of massive flames and ensuing mail bombs due to not playing nice online. Those who have giggled at this advice down the road have regretted doing so.

What are discussion forums or newsgroups?

Discussion groups and newsgroups are areas on the Internet where people discuss every possible topic you can imagine via private e-mail and gigantic message boards. Google has a great way to navigate the newsgroups based on your area of interest at http://groups.google.com. There are tens of thousands of groups where one can post a message, comment, or question about almost any topic you can imagine. Those who frequent a newsgroup can respond by posting a message or article to you via e-mail and/or to the group publicly. For example chi.general is the Chicago general discussion newsgroup. General topics about Chicago are discussed there. Chi.internet is where people discuss issues involving Chicago Internet related topics—only! In these discussion areas, it is expected that you only post a message or an article pertaining to the topic of the newsgroup and that you follow that newsgroups rules or charter. For example, I have discussion boards at NetiquetteForums.com where you can do the same on the topic of Netiquette.

Each newsgroup or discussion forum has a "charter" or set of rules which will be posted on a regular basis. Read it and follow the guidelines if you want to become part of that community. Take note of the rules governing the newsgroup and behave accordingly. If you want to be part of that group, you need to follow their rules. If you don't like or intend on following the rules, then don't join in the first place and upset the experience for other members of the group. When it comes to rules, just as in the off-line world, the rules are established and generally not open for discussion. It is a good idea to be a lurker for a while before joining in any conversations. A lurker is one who initially just reads postings without responding to the group. By doing this you get a feel for the personality of the group, who the regulars are, and what is tolerated and what isn't. If you break the charter or post off topic, you will get e-mails noting the error of your ways—guaranteed! At that point, offer your humble apologies and cancel the message.

What is the best way to e-mail a resume?
This will be a breeze, so relax and save your nerves for the face-to-face interview! ;-) First make sure your resume is saved in .txt or .rtf format. These are formats that are standard and readable by most computer systems. By saving your resume in text (.txt) or rich-text format (.rft) only, will show you have an understanding of technology. If you send a Word document and the employer has Microsoft Works depending on each side's versions, they may not be able to open your resume. If they can covert your Word document, it may not lay out as you intended therefore not giving the

best impression possible. Text and rich-text format help prevent this problem.

Some companies allow you to submit your resume in HTML. Usually a company will be clear about the format required. First, compose your e-mail cover message. Look for a menu item named "Attachment" or a paper-clip icon in your e-mail program. By clicking on that item, a list of directories and files on your hard drive will be available. Look for the file you would like to attach and select it. Viola! When you press Send, the file is automatically sent with the e-mail. Before sending off an important file like your resume, do a test first and send the file to yourself at your e-mail address. You can then view how the resume will look on the other end. Make sure the file isn't over two hundred kilobytes in size. If it is, use a compression program so that you don't fill up the potential employers' e-mail inbox with an overly large file. And it should go without saying, always spell check!

What does it mean when I see that Web sites were designed for 800x600?

Many thirteen- to fifteen-inch monitors used to have a factory setting for the monitor's resolution set at 640x480. This calls out the amount of pixels used to display images on your screen. In the beginning smart Webmasters took this into consideration when developing Web sites. Now, increasingly this default is now 800x600. You can change your resolution to 800x600 or 1024x768—the more pixels the smaller the display by going into your Control Panel and choosing Display. Larger monitors are more conducive to 1024x768 because you have more screen space; however, you can change your monitor's settings to your personal taste. Keep in mind that when deviating from the current standard of 800x600, some Web sites may layout differently and could not display as intended.

COMMON E-MAIL ACRONYMS

Acronym: Abbreviations of commonly used phrases as used in e-mail. Acronyms are not an excuse to not spell out words or to type cryptically. There is a time and place for their use, and they should be used sparingly and only when appropriate (i.e., not in your resume). Below are some typical acronyms you will encounter in your online communications.

Once online for even a short time you will find an acronym for almost any situation. To get you started, here is a list of the most commonly acronyms used in e-mail, message boards, and IM.

ACRONYM	MEANING
AFAIK	As Far As I Know
BBL	Be Back Later
BFN	Bye for Now
BRB	Be Right Back
BTW	By The Way
FUBAR	"Fixed" Up Beyond All Recognition
FB	Files Busy
FWIW	For What It's Worth
FYI	For Your Information
g	Grin(usually in brackets)
gd&h	grinning, ducking, and hiding
gd&r	grinning, ducking, and running
gd&r,vvf	grinning, ducking, and running,

	very, very fast
HSIK	How Should I Know
IAE	In Any Event
IANAL	I Am Not A Lawyer
IMO	In My Opinion
IMHO	In My Humble Opinion
IOW	In Other Words
JFYI	Just For Your Information
LOL	Laughing Out Loud
	(or Laughing On Line)
LMAO	Laughing My—Off
NBD	No Big Deal
NOYB	None Of Your Business
OIC	Oh, I See
OTL	Out To Lunch
OTOH	On The Other Hand
PITA	Pain In The A—
PMFJI	Pardon Me For Jumping In
PTB	Powers That Be
RSN	Real Soon Now
RTFM	Read The "Fine" Manual
S	Smile (big *S*, small *s*)
TANJ	There Ain't No Justice
TANSTAAFL	There Ain't No Such Thing
	As A Free Lunch
TIA	Thanks In Advance
TIC	Tongue In Cheek
TPTB	The Powers That Be
TTFN	Ta Ta For Now
TTYL	Talk To You Later
TYVM	Thank You Very Much
VBG	Very Big Grin
WOA	Work Of Art
WTH	What The H—
WYSIWYG	What You See Is What You Get

COMMON E-MAIL EMOTICONS

Emoticon: A figure created in e-mail using the symbols on the keyboard. Read with the head tilted to the left. Used to convey the spirit in which a line of text is typed. With e-mail you will communicate with people who may not know you; they cannot see your facial expressions or body language. This lends to the misunderstandings which I get contacted about for advice all the time. Also known as "smileys" these symbols will help others know where you are coming from and to make the intent of your typed comments clear. If you don't use Emoticons and your e-mail is misunderstood, it is your own fault.

Here, I have listed some of the most common as well as those only for comic relief:

EMOTICON	MEANING
:-I	Semi-smiley
:-%	User has a beard
:-=)	Older user with mustache
:-\	Undecided user
:-p	User is sticking their tongue out (at you!)
:-'|	User has a cold
:-)8	User is dressed up
:-D	User has a big mouth
:-#	User's lips are sealed.

:-o	User is shocked, surprised.
:-s	User after a *bizarre* comment.
:-{	User has a mustache
:-|	No-expression face, "that comment doesn't faze me"
-:-)	User sports a mohawk and admires Mr. T
:^$	Put your money where your mouth is
:-&	User which is tongue-tied
:-9	User licking its lips
:-(	Sad
:-X	User is wearing a bow tie
:-7	User after a wry statement
:-@	User is screaming
:-%	User is a banker
:-)	Humor (or smiley)
:-))	Big smile or grin
:-c	Bummed-out smiley
:-Q	Smoker
;-)	Winking smiley
(-:	User is left-handed
{(:-)	User is wearing toupee
+-(:-)	User is the pope
*:o)	User is a bozo
*<|:-)	User is Santa Claus (ho ho ho)
]:-}>	User is a "little devil"
=:-)	Smiley punk rocker
|-)	User is asleep (boredom)
8-)	User wears glasses
8:-)	Glasses on forehead
o-)	User is a Cyclops
{	User is Alfred Hitchcock
@-}—}—	A rose

INTERNET GLOSSARY

Here is a collection of some of the terms you may run into during your online activities. In addition, some of the terminology listed will give you a brief history of the Internet and World Wide Web that you were not aware of.

ARPA: This stands for Advanced Research Projects Agency, an arm of the U.S. Department of Defense, and the agency that created the ARPAnet.

ARPAnet: A network started in the 1960s by the Advanced Research Projects Agency (ARPA) to connect several research institutions and laboratories. The goal was two-fold: first, to coordinate research among similar labs; and second, to create a completely decentralized network. The Department of Defense wanted a network that could withstand a nuclear attack on the United States. Because the net is decentralized, there is no central computer to knock out. In recent years, this has been both a burden and a help. On one hand, no censorship can occur (except as unwritten rules enforced by the users themselves). But on the other hand, the Internet's growth has made it increasingly difficult to find anything. Unlike the local phone company, it is nearly impossible to find a complete "white pages," since there is no central governing body to catalog the net's features. (By the way, the ARPAnet was turned off in 1986. It was a miracle of decentralization that, when ARPAnet was shut down, no one but the system operators knew about it.)

ASCII: The American Standard Code for Information Interchange, a standard way of representing text. ASCII text contains no formatting. This makes it handy for sending among computers on multiple platforms e.g., between IBMs and Macs. ASCII is the standard language of Internet e-mail and newsgroup text, among other things.

Browser: A program used to view World Wide Web pages. Most Web browsers also can access WAIS, Gopher, FTP, and telnet. The browser reads the HTML and other programming codes to display the pages as you see them. Microsoft Internet Explorer, Mozilla, Opera, and Netscape are the most popular browsers.

Cache: The cache file in your browser remembers every Web site you have been to. This enables you to keep clicking on the browser's Back button to go to the pages you were at previously without waiting for them to have to download again. If you are not going to use the information in this file after you log off, it is a good idea to get in the habit of clearing out the cache at the end of every session. Many browsers also allow you to determine the cache size and when it should be cleared.

CERN: The European Center for Nuclear Research, the organization that created the World Wide Web in 1989. Remember this the next time you play trivial pursuit!

DNS: The Domain Name System, a standard way of stating Internet addresses. There are specific ending addresses called "top-level domains," such as "com" depending upon what the address refers to. Below are the most commonly used domain suffixes; however, now there is a suffix for almost every country on the planet Earth.

EXAMPLE DOMAIN SUFFIX	STANDS FOR:
.edu	Educational Institution
.org	Nonprofit Organization
.gov	Government Organization
.com	Commercial
.biz	Business
.ws	World Site
.us	United States
.mil	Military Address
.ca	In Canada
.cn	In China
.fr	In France
.de	In Germany
.uk	In the United Kingdom

Emoticon ("Smiley"): Certain characters that some people use to help express emotion in e-mail. The most common is :-). With a little imagination and a tilt of your head, you may see that this is a smiley face. All of these faces are to help express different emotions with recent programs now available that offer little smiley graphics in lieu of their plain text counterparts. It is important when you e-mail, that you use emoticons to relay the tone of your e-mail. If you crack a joke and don't utilize a smiley, the other party may not know you are joking and may misinterpret your e-mail.

FAQ: Stands for **F**requently **A**sked **Q**uestions and is a common term used on the Internet. When visiting a Web site looking for information, the first place to check out is the Web site's FAQ. Most likely many of your questions, which have been asked by previous visitors, will be listed for your reference.

Flame/Flame War: A very harsh message from one person to another, mostly in newsgroups. Flames are often directed at newbies or those who are being troublemakers. The harshness in them is usually not intelligent commentary or a debate on a difference of opinion. Normally, it is just an insult hurled by a jerk who does not know how to communicate civilly and with clarity. Huge "flame wars" can often erupt around volatile issues. It is always best to avoid these situations as continuing the "conversation" is unlikely to change anyone's opinion. What we learned from our mothers applies here: "If you can't say something nice don't say anything at all."

Freeware: Free software. Also see shareware and public domain.

FTP: File Transfer Protocol. This is one standardized way of transmitting files on the Internet. As with most services on the Internet, there are specific FTP servers containing specific types of files. Due to the popularity of technology in the last decade, FTP has now become a verb. As an example, you will hear people say "FTP it to your computer."

Home Page: A space on the World Wide Web where companies and individuals gave information posted about themselves. Many people and businesses refer to their Web Sites as their Home Page. Increasingly, however, "home page" is now more likely to be used in the context of a personal noncommercial Web site.

HTML: Hypertext Markup Language is the standard way in which all World Wide Web pages are written. It is read using browsers such as Opera, Mozilla, Netscape, and Microsoft Internet Explorer.

HTTP: Hypertext Transfer Protocol. Much like FTP, this is just another way of sending material across the global network. HTTP is specifically used to send World Wide Web pages across the Internet.

IRC: Internet Relay Chat is a method of conducting live chats on the Internet. It is sort of like a CB radio, in that people can choose whichever channel they want and then chat with whoever is on that channel. This can mean thousands of people chatting at once. At times this is practically unmanageable and not very enjoyable. Many Web sites now offer chats where additional software or plugins is not necessary.

Link: Whenever text on a Web page is in a different color than the majority of text, and is underlined, or changes colors when your mouse pointer hovers over it, this is referred to as a link. Links can take you to another area at that Web site or to another site on the Web. When you click on a link, your browser will take you to the designated place the link calls out. You will notice that most links will change to a different color once you click on them. This is a visual to you to let you know you have "been there, done that."

Lurker or Lurking: A lurker is one who reads postings in forums or newsgroups without responding or participating. Before jumping into any discussion area, initially it is a good idea to be a lurker before posting to determine the rules and personality of the group. Don't want to unnecessarily step on any toes now, do we?

Mailing List: A subject discussion area that is much like a newsgroup. The main difference between a mailing list and a newsgroup is that a mailing list is performed by e-mail, while newsgroups are not. People send messages about topics to a central computer, and then the mailing list program distributes the message to everyone who has subscribed to the list.

MIME: Multipurpose Internet Mail Extensions is a protocol for attaching nontext files (e.g., graphics or programs) to e-mail messages. The only caveat to sending a MIME message is that the person receiving the message must have a MIME-compatible mail program (or MIME decoder), as well. Not all mail programs support MIME.

NCSA: The National Center for Supercomputing Applications at the University of Illinois at Urbana-Champaign.

Netizen: A term used to describe an Internet user who is aware of the culture and rules governing the Internet.

NETiquette: Derived from the two words *Net*work and *Eti-quette,* these are the rules of participation online. The Internet from the start has been a self-governing society. Knowing what is tolerated and/or allowed by the Internet Community will help you avoid being flamed.

Newbie: A somewhat derogatory term on the Internet meaning an inexperienced and obnoxious new user. The term refers to the brand of user who is unschooled in the Internet's traditions, takes little time to learn them, and acts rudely.

Newsgroups: Another area on the Internet where you can post questions or join discussions. Google groups, located at http://groups.google.com, is where most onliners tap into the Internet newsgroups. Some quick rules to remember:

- When joining a new newsgroup, watch the flow of messages for a few days to discern the group's customs before contributing messages. This is called lurking.

- Do not promote any product you will commercially gain from in any way. Internet users have tried very hard to avoid commercialization since the Internet's inception, and they do not appreciate any deviation from this un-

written rule in discussion groups. Send out an unsolicited e-mail and you could possibly receive thousands
of flames. Enough to shut down your server or have
your ISP cancel your account.

- Keep messages short and on topic.

- Never post the same message to more than one
  newsgroup, especially if it's a file. There are some
  users who read many newsgroups daily and don't appreciate reading the same message, or getting the
  same file, more than once.

- Be sure to review this book and OnlineNetiquette.com
  in its entirety before you send your first post.

NSF: National Science Foundation, the agency which
founded the NSFNET.

NSFnet: One of the "backbone networks" of the Internet.

PPP: An abbreviation for Point-to-Point Protocol, a standard
for connecting modems, specifically, to the Internet. It is
the successor to SLIP.

Phishing: Phishing is a scam that uses spam to deceive
consumers into disclosing their personal information.
Phishing is considered a two-step scam. First it steals a
company's identity and then uses the information to vic-
timize consumers by stealing their credit identities.

Public Domain: While freeware is cost-free, the actual code
to public-domain software is available to anyone who
wants it. Public-domain software has been refined and
modified possibly hundreds of times by people who have
the ability to improve it.

Search Engine: A search engine, such Google, is sort of the online version of the yellow pages. By learning each search engine's criteria for searching the Web, you can effectively type in keyword phrases that allow the search engine to pull up a list of all the Web pages that list the information you are looking for. Each search engine operates differently, and each has a section at their site that instructs you on how to use their features for the most accurate outcome.

Server: A central computer from which a particular service takes place. For example, there are FTP servers, Gopher servers, and WAIS servers. Servers are accessed by clients (software).

Shareware: Software for which users must pay a fee after a certain trial period. The trial period is usually thirty days, and the fee is normally lower than the cost of commercial software. Most unregistered shareware is only available in a less-powerful version, with the full version available upon registration. It is strongly recommended that if you like the software and plan on using it, pay for it!

SLIP: An abbreviation for Serial Line Interface Protocol. SLIP is a standard for connecting modems, specifically, to the Internet. It has rapidly been succeeded by PPP.

Snail Mail: The online reference to U.S. Postal Mail. Too funny! ;-)

Spam: This term refers to multiple e-mails sent to those who are not interested in what they have to offer. Compare spam to the junk mail you receive in your snail-mail box. It is strongly suggested that you never send unsolicited e-mail to anyone either directly or through their Web site's form. You will get flamed and you may even lose your

ISP account as many Internet service providers will disconnect you when they receive complaints about your spamming activities. You can count on other Netizens complaining to your ISP. This practice is not tolerated by the Internet Community as a whole.

Status Bar: This bar at the bottom of your browser's window always indicates the status of your request. It indicates what percentage of the page, file, or graphic being downloaded. Your status bar will reflect "Done" when the downloading is completed.

TCP/IP: The standard for communication among computers connected to the Internet and stands for Transmission Control Protocol/Internet Protocol. While it is a relatively slow protocol, it works wonders for intercommunication among different systems.

UNIX: A standard for network operating systems. UNIX has been around for decades and comes in many flavors. For the Internet user, the most common contact with UNIX is the way in which directories are divided. All UNIX directories are separated by forward slashes. For example, "myfiles/mydocuments" might be a directory. Also be aware that UNIX directories are case sensitive; *myfiles* is different, in UNIX, than *MyFiles*. Get in the habit when writing down URLs or e-mail addresses to underline the letters that may be capitalized. In general, most URLs and e-mail addresses will always work when typed in all-small case.

URL: Universal or Uniform Resource Locator. A standard way of representing services on the Internet. A URL usually consists of a scheme name (such as HTTP), followed by a colon, two slashes, and then the address of the site to which you would like to connect.

USENET Newsgroup: A place on the Internet where people can discuss pretty much any topic. Google has fully integrated the past twenty years of Usenet archives into Google groups, which now offers access to more than 845 million messages dating back to 1981.

UUEncode/UUDecode: A method of putting binary files (graphics and/or programs) into an Internet e-mail or newsgroup message.

INDEX

"

"phishing"
  warning against disclosing
    information such as
    account numbers, 144
"technology mushroom"
  ("shroom"), 59

A

acronyms
  commonly used. *See* under
    e-mail
  proper and polite use of, 38
all caps, 10, 13
  avoiding, 15, 79, 163
ASCII, 70, 88
  ASCII coding to deter spam,
    112
attachments, 9
  and viruses, 28, 124
  courtesy in sending, 25, 46,
    72, 118
  forwarding, 102
  in business e-mail, 82
  sending, 167

B

browser software, 162
bugs and viruses, 27, 121
business e-mails, 78
  formatting, 82
  use of e-mail fields, 81
  use of signature files, 85

C

colors, avoid in signature files,
  88
cookies, 151
copyright
  private e-mail, 24
  Web graphics and content,
    161
cyberparenting, 75

D

discussion forums, 165
domains, 130
  domain slamming, 133
  ICANN (Internet Corporation
    for Assigned Names and
    Numbers)
    umbers), 132
  whois feature, 135
down editing, 41, 84, 102

E

e-cards and e-greetings, 127
e-mail
  acronyms, 168. *See also*
    acronyms
  background colors/images,
    16
  carbon copy, 16
  clarity and accuracy in
    communicating, 32
  color coding, 100
  emoticons, 170

notes on forwarding, 102
organizing, 97
responding to, 41
rude e-mails, 92
sending files (attachments),
    71
text color, 16
word choice, 50
e-mail greetings, 30, 85
emoticons
    commonly used. *See* under
    e-mail

F

FAQ (Frequently Asked
    Questions), 160
files
    documents and spread-
    sheets, 69
    file extensions, 67
    naming, 67
    organizing, 73
    the 8.3 pattern, 68
filters, 98, 99, 100, 110, 111,
    117
flames, 165

H

html e-mails, 148

I

instant messaging (IM), 37
    use for business, 39
ISP (Internet Service Provider),
    25, 47
    definition, 161
    difference from online ser-
    vices, 161
    reporting abusive e-mail to,
    56
    TOS (Terms of Service), 94

L

lowercase letters, better
    readability, 15

M

mail bomb, 49

N

netiquette, definition of, 9
newsgroups. *See* discussion
    forums

O

online employment
    opportunities, 155
    avoiding color and formatting
    in resumes, 156
    resume, 166

P

personal information, caution in
    disclosing, 20

R

resolution, 167
return receipt request, avoid
    using of, 22

S

search engines, 162
search tips, 158
spam (or Unsolicited
    Commercial E-mail), 45,
    85, 164
    autoresponders, 107
    how not to look spammy, 117
    identifying and handling, 104
    spammers and service
    providers, 104

subscriptions, 113
tips to stop, 111
SpamCop, 115

T

Trojan Horse, 124
trolling, 24, 54

U

URL (Uniform Resource
    Locator), 68, 86
definition, 163
spammers nonuse of URLs,
    108
use in "phishing", 144

V

virus, 27, 120, 121
and attachments, 84
and spam, 107
definition, 122
effect on computers, 123
files that spread, 122
in e-mail, 27
protection, 28, 120, 125
software, 26, 121
spread of, 123
susceptibility of Microsoft
    Outlook users, 27, 121,
    149
warnings, 10, 18, 26

Z

zipping files, 24

www.ingramcontent.com/pod-product-compliance
Lightning Source LLC
Chambersburg PA
CBHW051239050326
40689CB00007B/989